5/14

PARENTS HAVE THE POWER
TO MAKE SPECIAL EDUCATION WORK

AN INSIDER GUIDE

JUDITH CANTY GRAVES AND CARSON GRAVES

FOREWORD BY ROBERT K. CRABTREE, ESQ.

Jessica Kingsley *Publishers*
London and Philadelphia

First published in 2014
by Jessica Kingsley Publishers
73 Collier Street
London N1 9BE, UK
and
400 Market Street, Suite 400
Philadelphia, PA 19106, USA

www.jkp.com

Library of Congress Cataloging in Publication Data
Graves, Judith Canty.
    Parents have the power to make special education work : an insider guide / Judith Canty Graves and Carson Graves.
      pages cm
Includes bibliographical references and index.
ISBN 978-1-84905-970-1 (alk. paper)
1. Special education--Parent participation. I. Title.
LC3969.G66 2014
371.9--dc23
                                201302454

British Library Cataloguing in Publication Data
A CIP catalogue record for this book is available from the British Library

ISBN 978 1 84905 970 1
eISBN 978 0 85700 878 7

Printed and bound in Great Britain by Bell & Bain Ltd, Glasgow

CONTENTS

FOREWORD

The book you hold in your hand offers a lucid and pragmatic guide ("pragmatic" being high praise from this grizzled old special education attorney!) through the maze of public and private procedures that parents must navigate to secure the services that their children with disabilities need. This excellent tool takes a well-earned place in a long chain of parent-to-parent resources meant to ensure that the promises written into state and federal statutes some forty years ago will be fulfilled.

A legal revolution began for children with disabilities and their parents in 1972, when the Massachusetts legislature enacted a special education reform act known as Chapter 766. A few years later, much of the model embodied in Chapter 766 was adopted in a 1975 federal statute called the Education for All Handicapped Children Act (EAHCA), later renamed the Individuals with Disabilities Education Act (IDEA).

These enactments spawned major changes in the basic structures, standards and programs of public education for students with disabilities. The changes raised an enormous challenge to the bureaucracies that would be called upon to implement them—primarily the public school districts, first of Massachusetts and then of the entire nation—and the prospect of those changes provoked significant resistance from those bureaucracies. It is unlikely that Chapter 766 and the later EAHCA could have been written into law without their advocates organizing a very deep and wide coalition of stakeholders to carry out the gritty work of convincing legislators to take the giant step those initiatives represented.

Two enormously important results of this process were the empowerment of a previously disenfranchised population and the creation of a new culture and community that united advocates and persons with disabilities across lines that had previously divided them—lines between types of disability, lines between schools of thought at odds over teaching approaches, lines between professionals and administrators who, before they came to argue about their roles and responsibilities, fundamentally agreed on their commitment to improving the lot of children with disabilities. In short, jealousies and battles for limited resources had to be set aside to achieve the victories represented in Chapter 766 and the EAHCA, and the resulting new community learned about moving together to gain common goals.

FOUR DECADES AGO: FERTILE GROUND FOR CHANGE

The movement in the early 1970s to expand and deepen the legal rights of children with disabilities in schools had its roots in the eloquent language of the U.S. Supreme Court written on behalf of another disenfranchised school population, children of color. In *Brown v. Board of Education* (1954), the Court declared the end of "separate but equal" as a viable platform for public education in a democratic society with these ringing words:

> Today, education is perhaps the most important function of state and local governments. Compulsory school attendance laws and the great expenditures for education both demonstrate our recognition of the importance of education to our democratic society. It is required in the performance of our most basic public responsibilities, even service in the armed forces. It is the very foundation of good citizenship. Today it is a principal instrument in awakening the child to cultural values, in preparing him for later professional training, and in helping him to adjust normally to his environment. In these days, it is doubtful that any child may reasonably be expected to succeed in life if he is denied the opportunity of an education. Such an opportunity, where the state has undertaken to provide it, is a right which must be made available to all on equal terms.[1]

In the spirit of *Brown*, some later courts extended the equal protection of law to children who had been excluded from school because of their disabilities. For example, a federal district court, ruling in favor of children who had been categorized as "mentally retarded," held in *PARC v. Pennsylvania* (1972) that: "It is the Commonwealth's obligation to place each mentally retarded child in a free, public program of education and training appropriate to the child's capacity ..."[2]

In another decision, *Mills v. Board of Education* (1972) a federal court held that children with disabilities could not legally be excluded from school because of their behaviors or for any other reason, including a claimed lack of sufficient resources to educate those children.

Decisions such as *PARC* and *Mills* explicitly referenced the language of *Brown*, but they were also certainly driven and informed as well by the philosophy and politics that led to the Civil Rights Act of 1964, enacted by Congress to extend the promise of equal opportunity to the descendants of slaves. The principles that drove these advances on behalf of citizens of color inevitably awakened other sectors of our population to the need to tear down whatever arbitrary and bigoted walls had kept them in a state of separate and clearly unequal exclusion from the benefits of our culture.

FRAGMENTATION AND EXCLUSION: THE MASSACHUSETTS CONTEXT

In Massachusetts one critical motivating factor that helped to prepare the ground for what ultimately became Chapter 766, was the realization by state legislators that there was a widespread problem facing many constituents that could not be resolved case by case in the usual manner of constituent service. Legislators' phones were ringing daily with calls from citizens whose children were poorly served in, or even totally excluded from, their public schools. A wider version of this pattern was experienced by Congressmen and Senators in Washington, preparing the ground there for enactment of the EAHCA.

What all those constituent calls reflected was, in part, the fragmentary and idiosyncratic nature of the laws that attempted to address the needs of children with disabilities. In Massachusetts, for example, separate statutes provided different kinds and levels of support to children with different disabilities, depending on the specific disability that had been identified. The resulting patchwork tended to reflect more the political savvy and organizing strength of the disability groups that had supported the various initiatives than any rational basis for distinguishing among those disabilities.

The results ranged from full funding for outside placements for some children, to 50 percent funding for outside placements for others, to zero support if a particular category of disability had not made its way into the statute books. Little attention was paid to the development of services within children's home school districts. Several categories of challenges went unaddressed altogether, including, significantly, those of children with multiple disabilities.

THE AIMS OF SPECIAL EDUCATION REFORM

The opening section of Chapter 766 outlined the need "for a flexible and uniform system of special education" that included a "non-discriminatory system for identifying and evaluating the individual needs of children requiring special education opportunities," "periodic evaluation of the benefit of the program to the child and the nature of the child's needs," and most importantly "to prevent denials of equal educational opportunity on the basis of national origin, sex, economic status, race, religion, and physical or mental handicap." In short, Chapter 766 was designed to provide "the opportunity for a full range of special education programs for children requiring [them]."

Then, in perhaps the most radical of its statements (at least as far as school administrators were concerned), the purpose section turned to the role of parents and advocates and declared the legislative aim of involving them directly in the identification, planning and oversight of services for students with disabilities:

> Recognizing, finally, that present inadequacies and inequities in the provision of special education services to children with special needs have resulted largely from a lack of significant parent and lay involvement in overseeing, evaluating and operating special education programs, this act is designed to build such involvement through the creation of regional and state advisory committees with significant powers and by specifying an accountable procedure for evaluating each child's special needs thoroughly before placement in a program and periodically thereafter.[3]

To ensure such involvement, the new statute went even further, as it provided for a due process system under which impartial adjudicators would hear and decide disputes between parents and school districts over the identification and provision of services to students with disabilities.

The EAHCA followed suit in 1975, inaugurating nationwide (as all states ultimately accepted funding under the statute) the right to due process and a decision by an impartial hearing officer and, by appeal if need be, a court regarding any issue arising under the Act.

ORGANIZING THEN AND NOW

The end result of these changes was also the creation of a broad and powerful community among parents and advocates of all description. Where parents of children with disabilities had previously stood and acted within their isolated groups, if indeed they united with others at all, they now had experienced a dissolution of barriers and perceived conflicting interests between advocacy groups—they had discovered the power of uniting and joining others in the common task of improving things for all children with disabilities.

Organizations today that stand as enduring examples of the power of uniting in the common interest include, for example: the Federation for Children With Special Needs in Boston (first formed as the "Coalition for Special Education Reform" uniting numerous previously independent advocacy organizations to develop and lobby for Chapter 766 and now a training and information resource for parents everywhere); the Massachusetts Advocates for Children (still studying and exposing the shortcomings of our public education systems' efforts to serve children with disabilities and other challenges as well as organizing and acting for change at the legislature, in court and in public discourse); and the national Council of Parent Attorneys and Advocates (COPAA), an extremely useful source of information on special education law and watchdog over the actions of Congress and states in the implementation of IDEA.

As the activities and resources of these and countless other organizations reaching back to the origins of civil rights for students with disabilities demonstrate, the actions of those who would strip away the rights that have been established for children with disabilities will never again be met with silence. Parents who once felt isolated and powerless need never return to that status.

EVOLUTION AND DEVOLUTION: A THOUSAND CUTS

The teachings of this parent guide need to be understood in the context of the forces that have steadily worked to undermine the high hopes parents and advocates had in the optimistic early days of Chapter 766 and the EAHCA. The rights and resources of students and parents have undeniably advanced far beyond the deprivation, fragmentation, and discrimination that existed before and, as noted, there is a solid, wide-spread and sustainable community in place to defend and, when possible, extend those rights and resources.

However, school departments, strapped for cash and anxious to preserve prerogatives, and the wider political forces whose interests are primarily to reduce the tax burden of educating children—and especially children with expensive needs—have chipped away at the statutes over the decades, seeking to interpret the words of state and federal special education law at the lowest possible level in order to minimize funds devoted to children with disabilities. These forces tap into and speak, however subtly, for the darker voices of humanity insofar as they represent prejudice against persons with disabilities and resentment against what they perceive as an unwarranted right to services that drain public coffers with little or no societal benefit.

Parents should accordingly enter the world of special education advocacy with a cool and clear understanding of the limits of the law and the advantages that school districts hold when parents ask for more than the district is willing to provide.

The first U.S. Supreme Court opinion interpreting the federal special education law, *Rowley v. Hendrick Hudson School District* (1984), declared school districts are required only to provide access and "some" educational benefit ("meaningful" or "effective" progress, as later court decisions indicated), rather than to educate children with disabilities to their maximum potential.[4] Later Supreme Court decisions: (1) effectively required parents to carry the burden of proof in most hearings brought under IDEA (*Schaffer v. Weast*, 2005) even though districts possess most of the evidence on which decisions must be made; (2) denied reimbursement for the fees charged by experts when parents prevail in proceedings under IDEA, even though most cases by far can only be won with the testimony of credible experts (*Arlington Central School District Board of Education v. Murphy*, 2006); and (3) in *Buckannon Board and Care Home, Inc. V. West Va. Dep't of Health and Human Resources* (2001), a decision affecting all federal civil rights statutes including ours, held that to "prevail" and thus be entitled to have a defendant reimburse one's reasonable attorneys' fees, a plaintiff must actually secure a favorable ruling by a judge (or hearing officer), thus reversing decades of a far more liberal interpretation of "prevailing" in most federal courts that had entitled plaintiffs to attorneys' fees even if they achieved a favorable result without having to pursue the case all the way to a hearing officer's or judge's order.

Some more favorable Supreme Court and other federal court decisions have confirmed parents' rights in a number of important areas. These include the right to obtain reimbursement of tuition and other costs if a school district does not provide a free appropriate public education under IDEA (*Burlington School Commitee V. Mass Department of Education*, 1985); a school district's responsibility to provide medical supports so long as the supports don't require the direct services of a physician (*Irving Independent School District V. Tatro*, 1984); and the right of states to provide a greater degree of protection or require a higher standard of services for children with disabilities than the federal law, IDEA (*David D. V. Dartmouth*, 1985). Despite these and other court decisions, on balance the climate that ultimately has been created by the interpretations of the courts, various revisions to state and federal law, the pressures of the economy, and negative attitudes toward persons with disabilities and the costs of meeting their needs has made parental advocacy a steep and rocky road. Ambiguities are typically resolved in favor of school districts; deference is paid to the choices districts make for teaching approaches, assignments of personnel, placement options, peer grouping and so forth; procedural mistakes made by districts are treated as harmless unless parents can prove that the procedural violations significantly undermined the child's progress; and parents must typically exhaust, inch by inch, the incremental enhancements a district may offer before they can achieve, if ever, a program that genuinely advances their child's interests.

THE BOTTOM LINE

Notwithstanding all my dark descriptions of the erosion of rights and hopes since 1972, parents who take the time to educate themselves about the process and train themselves with the help of manuals like this one can make tremendous gains in their advocacy for their children. Take advantage, too, of the writing and training programs offered by advocacy organizations in your area. For example, Pete Wright's seminars and training programs (see www.wrightslaw.com), offered regularly around the country, can be a great resource to learn the fundamentals and keep up with changes in the law and new interpretations as courts continue to wrestle with its meaning and applications. Ally yourself with others who share your concerns and needs: advocacy groups organized around the particular challenges experienced by your child; local parent advisory groups monitoring your district's special education system; and other parents in your community whom you come to know as your child progresses through the system. All are sources of information and many can be sources of personal support and united influence under the right circumstances.

Finally, as this book so eloquently advises, understand that the battle is a long one that calls for patience, calmness, and persistence; continuing self-education; a realistic understanding of the limits of the law; and pragmatism. The system prefers the least intensive, most mainstreamed (least "restrictive") appropriate program and placement. It is not built to grant any child the best services that can be provided. Parents must be prepared to prioritize their wishes and, with the help of believable experts, make their way through the squares inch by inch, until either the district is meeting their child's needs or they have a fighting chance to prove that it cannot do so and must therefore support an alternative program.

Read this book and keep it handy for frequent reference! And may you, with its help, fight your way to a fantastic program for your child!

Robert K. Crabtree, Esq.

Mr. Crabtree, along with his later law partner, Lawrence Kotin, drafted much of the Massachusetts Special Education Reform Act, Chapter 766, that became a model for the federal special education law now known as the Individuals With Disabilities Education Act (IDEA). In 1981 they founded the Boston law firm, Kotin, Crabtree & Strong, LLP, and have maintained since then, within that general practice, a group devoted to representing parents and persons with disabilities. In 2005, Crabtree and Kotin were co-recipients of the Ziegler Founder's Award, given by the Federation for Children With Special Needs for their leadership in the formation of Chapter 766 and their decades of dedication to students with disabilities and their families.

ACKNOWLEDGMENTS

The authors would like to thank the many people who contributed their knowledge and support to this project. It would be impossible to overestimate how important these people were to making this book possible. Diane Love, Claire Canty, Kay Dowd, Margo Melnicove, William Strong, Eugene Ham, William T. Graves, Linda Segal, and Lisa Underkoffler, all reviewed early drafts and made invaluable suggestions. Also, we would like to thank Jessica Kingsley Publishers, especially our editor, Rachel Menzies, who had enough faith in our project to help us see it into production.

Three people in particular deserve special thanks for lending their insight, expertise, and significant effort to our project: Jason McCormack, the best neuropsychologist we have ever worked with; Noreen Curran, advocate extraordinaire; and Eileen Hagerty of the firm Kotin, Crabtree & Strong, LLP, who possesses a rare passion for both special education law and the English language. They "had our backs" in making sure that not only were we accurate in what we wrote, but wrote it in a clear and concise manner. Any failures of accuracy or clarity are completely the authors' and not of these wonderful and caring professionals.

Finally, we would like to acknowledge Robert Crabtree for graciously contributing an eloquent and thoughtful foreword. As someone who was "there at the beginning," he speaks with both authority and understanding of the history and current state of special education.

PREFACE

Almost 30 years of research and experience has demonstrated that the education of children with disabilities can be made more effective by strengthening the role and responsibility of parents.

—Office of Special Education and Rehabilitative
Services, U.S. Department of Education, 2010

We entered the world of special education like most parents, with concerns about our child and a diagnosis we didn't understand. Our experience began in preschool and continued through high school graduation, a span of 15 years. Over these years we met many other parents of children receiving special education services. We listened to their stories and heard many themes emerge that corresponded with our own observations. As a result of this experience, we can write with certainty that every single year of a child's education matters and that parents are the only constant advocates their child will have during these years. It is an enormous responsibility, but it can ultimately be a rewarding one.

One lesson our experience taught us is that the more parents know about special education, the more effective they can be as advocates for their children. Learning how special education works takes persistence because, like an iceberg, most of it exists below the surface of what parents can initially see. We have heard stories of school districts that are reasonable to deal with, but you are probably reading this book because you have encountered problems that may be preventing your child from receiving an education appropriate to his or her needs. The keys to overcoming these problems are knowledge and organization. The tools you will use are research and a network of carefully selected professionals and like-minded parents whom you must identify and cultivate.

We have come to realize that parents of children with special needs have two roles. The first, and most obvious role, is understanding and dealing with their child's unique disability. The second, and more subtle role, is learning to navigate around the icebergs of special education. This second role usually comes as a surprise. Parents who have quite naturally focused solely on their child's disability are often not prepared for how the special education system works. They assume that school personnel are the professionals who will know, and more importantly will do, what is best for their child. This assumption is all too often misplaced, because special education in many school districts has become an elaborate bureaucratic maze in which budget requirements are more important than doing what is right or even what is legally required. The result is confusion, disappointment, and lost opportunities.

This book is both a narrative of our personal experience navigating the special education system and a guide to help parents translate our experience to fit their own situation. When we entered special education in the early 1990s, there were no online search engines or social networking sites, so it was difficult to find information and meet other parents with similar concerns. We felt isolated and confused. A book like this would have changed our lives. That is why we wrote it, so that parents who are now involved with special education can learn from our experience. The realization that parents have the power to make special education work came to us while attending a workshop on transition planning. The speaker made the point that at a Team meeting most of the school personnel in the room actually knew very little about special education. Many understood individual pieces, depending on their specialties, but only the parents were in the position to see the whole picture. The workshop speaker encouraged parents to study the special education process, especially the laws, in order to understand their rights and protections and what a school district's obligations are to a student, because ultimately, it is the parents' responsibility for making sure that schools comply with the law. As the saying goes, knowledge is power.

Our message is that parents can make special education work if they take the time to understand their child's disability, their legal rights, and the often hidden agenda of school culture. We know that you, the parents, are the best advocates for your child. You must be proactive and organized, study the state and federal laws, and persevere. Doing all this will give you the information, the confidence, and the power to help your child get an appropriate education that will pay many dividends in the future. This will be the most important and rewarding job you will ever have. We hope this book will guide you and inspire you.

HOW TO USE THIS BOOK

We have written each chapter in the order that most parents encounter special education, from initial eligibility evaluations to transition planning and graduation from high school. For that reason, most readers may want to read the chapters in order. We have also included cross references to information mentioned in one chapter but explained in more detail in another. That way, readers can use the table of contents or index to go directly to a topic that interests them without having to read through a lot of preliminary text that may not be relevant to their current needs.

At the end of each chapter is a section titled "What parents can do." This is a list of suggestions on how readers can apply the information in that chapter to their individual situation. Just as every child is unique, every family dealing with special education has different needs.

Finally, no book can accurately claim to be a comprehensive guide to special education. There are too many aspects to consider, from the medical diagnosis of a disability, to the constantly changing state and federal laws, to the pressures and frustrations of dealing with the special education bureaucracy. To this end, we have included a list of special education books and websites that we have found helpful in Appendix C, "Resources."

THREE IMPORTANT ACRONYMS

Special education is full of specialized vocabulary and confusing acronyms. We have tried to avoid using these terms as much as possible, and where unavoidable have tried to explain these terms as clearly as we can. The following three acronyms, however, are so central to discussing special education that it is important to learn them before you start reading the text.

- *IDEA (Individuals with Disabilities Education Act):* This is the landmark federal law that defines the requirements for special education. The law has been revised and re-authorized several times since its initial passage in 1975 as the Education for All Handicapped Children Act, most recently in 2004. In addition to the acronym, Congressional acts are sometimes identified by their revision date. For example, the 2004 re-authorization of IDEA is frequently referred to as IDEA-04.

- *FAPE (Free Appropriate Public Education):* FAPE is what the Individuals With Disabilities Education Act guarantees children with qualifying disabilities. It means that special education services are provided at public expense and under public supervision and direction, and that the services meet all state and federal requirements, and comply with a student's Individualized Education Program. Having students with disabilities obtain FAPE is the purpose of all special education laws. Note the words "appropriate education." The law does not promise the "best education" for students in special education.

- *IEP (Individualized Education Program, or sometimes Individualized Education Plan):* This is a document, updated each year, that specifies what services a child in the special education system will receive. It is a legal contract between the school and the parents (or student if over 18 and is his or her own guardian). The IEP is regarded as the cornerstone of special education.

For a more complete list of acronyms and terms used in special education, see the glossary in Appendix B.

DISCLAIMER

This book is written from a parent's perspective. We are not attorneys, educators, or clinicians. Our interpretation of special education law, educational practices, and psychological testing is based on our own experience and opinion about what is best for students and their families. While qualified professionals have reviewed pertinent sections of the text for accuracy, this book is in no way intended to serve as a substitute for obtaining professional advice. Citations of the law are given purely for informational purposes and to provide a context for our opinions. In addition, special education law in some states supersedes federal laws.

The descriptions of interactions with our school system are based on letters, emails, and documents we have received. While our experience with special education occurred in the state of Massachusetts, our intent is to illustrate behavior that we believe is common to many school systems throughout the country. These descriptions are not meant to single out individuals or a particular school district. For that reason we have refrained from providing any identifying information that would distract from the points we are making.

Judith Canty Graves
Carson Graves

INTRODUCTION

Special education has evolved in the United States, just as society's understanding of people with disabilities has evolved. As with other aspects of our society, however, special education is subject to the pressures of economics and the influence of political expediency, both of which ultimately control the choices society makes about it. To better understand the parent's role in special education, it is instructive to briefly review how the concept of special education has developed over the past 200 years, examine the laws that govern special education in this country, and speculate on how current trends might affect special education in the future.

THE BEGINNINGS OF SPECIAL EDUCATION

Many historians cite the work of the physician Jean Marc Gaspard Itard with Victor, the "wild boy of Aveyron," as the first attempt at special education.[5] In late 18th century France, an approximately 12-year-old boy, Victor as he became known, was found living alone and naked in the woods, without the ability to speak, wear clothes, or live in a house. Scientists of the day felt that by studying Victor and educating him, they could learn much about what separated man from animals. After many unsuccessful attempts, a young medical student named Jean Marc Gaspard Itard took Victor into his home and spent many years attempting to socialize him and teach him language skills. According to Itard's reports, Victor was never able to progress beyond learning a few words and, while Victor adapted to living with other humans, his progress in that area was limited. In the context of special education, it is fair to say that Itard's attempts to educate Victor and integrate him into French society were decidedly mixed.

Probably the most famous and successful early special education teacher in the United States was Anne Sullivan Macy, the "miracle worker" who taught Helen Keller to communicate through sign language. Sullivan's ability to teach Keller, who was both deaf and blind and had no previous concept that objects and words were connected, is still inspirational today. From the 1950s to 2010, multiple television shows, Broadway plays, and motion pictures, have portrayed this remarkable relationship between student and teacher, the 1962 film winning two Academy Awards.[6]

In the latter part of the 19th and the first half of the 20th century, it was physicians and clergy rather than the public schools who addressed the educational needs of students with disabilities. Physicians Edouard O. Seguin and Samuel Gridley Howe and clergyman Thomas Hopkins Gallaudet disagreed with the 19th century notion that people with disabilities should be isolated in institutions. Instead, they believed that with proper education, people with disabilities could become productive members of society. Howe, in particular, argued that the instructional setting could, by itself, have a significant impact on the success or failure of the outcome. He and other early advocates of special education are generally given credit for the idea that special education should best take place within the structure of general education, what today is called inclusion, or "mainstreaming."

Mainstreaming was the predominant approach in educational theory initially, but there were other educators who believed that the most effective techniques for teaching students with disabilities were varied and needed to be applied with regard to the individual's specific disabilities. The general education environment, they felt, does not have the flexibility to properly implement these "best practices," thus potentially denying students with disabilities an education that was appropriate to the individual.*

The influence of educators who promoted mainstreaming lasted until after World War II, when the parents of children with special needs began to organize advocacy groups. One of the first was the American Association on Mental Deficiency, founded in 1947. This parent-organized group, and others like it, began to highlight flaws in the mainstreaming concept. One of the biggest problems, the parent groups argued, was that mainstream classroom teachers lacked adequate training in the most effective methods for teaching students with disabilities. These groups advocated for more educators specially trained to teach these students.

---

* What is the best environment in which special education should take place is still an open question today. For a more detailed discussion of this topic, see the sections "FAPE and LRE" and "A closer look at the law" in Chapter 1, "Getting Started in Special Education."

Additional support for the idea that students with disabilities had a right to the same educational opportunities as their non-disabled peers came from the civil rights movement of the 1950s and 1960s. As a result, the level of school participation for the disabled increased at both the state and local levels. Despite this progress, by 1970 only 20 percent of students with identified disabilities were being educated in public schools. In fact, many state laws still specifically excluded students who were deaf, blind, "mentally retarded," or "emotionally disturbed" from getting any public education at all. Clearly, something more than public understanding was needed.

DEVELOPMENT OF STATE AND FEDERAL LAWS

Massachusetts was the first state to pass a comprehensive special education law, known as Chapter 766, in 1974. Both Chapter 766 and Chapter 74, another law passed the same year, attempted to get local school systems to provide special education services in a cost-effective manner by combining resources with other school systems to form educational collaboratives. The intention was that these collaboratives could provide a full range of services to students with special needs in the areas of academics, vocational education, staff development, research, and innovative programs.

At the federal level, the first legal recognition of the rights of students with disabilities occurred in 1975 when Congress passed the Education for All Handicapped Children Act (EHA or EAHCA). This law was modeled after Massachusetts' Chapter 766. For states that accepted federal funding under the EHA, the statute required public schools to provide a "free appropriate public education" (FAPE) to students with a wide range of disabilities. It also required that school districts provide this education in the "least restrictive environment" (LRE) possible, a mandate that opened the doors of mainstream classrooms to the 80 percent of students with special needs who had up to then been excluded.

Individuals with Disabilities Education Act (IDEA)

In 1983, the EHA was expanded to include provisions for training parents and to establish information centers at the state level. In 1986, the EHA was expanded again to add early intervention programs for infants and additional services for preschoolers. In 1990, the law was revised yet again and renamed the Individuals with Disabilities Education Act (IDEA). IDEA was re-authorized in 1997 and revised to place an emphasis on access to the general school curriculum. In 2004, during the next re-authorization of IDEA, the law made a number of changes regarding teacher qualifications, procedural safeguards and how IEP goals are written, among others.

The point of these laws was to raise the level of academic and social benefit for students with special needs and overcome the low expectations that educators generally had. The emphasis on inclusion into the general school community was seen as a progressive step. It kept students with disabilities out of institutions and gave them a place in public schools, so that students with special education needs would have the opportunity to meet the educational standards that apply to all children. As more and more disabilities were diagnosed, however, students who were already part of the school community began to be recognized as also needing special education services. These were the students who didn't fit into the typical mold and were bullied and ostracized because their disabilities weren't visible. Some of them needed a separate environment where they could strengthen their abilities and flourish.

IDEA COMPARED TO STATE SPECIAL EDUCATION LAWS
Most states have special education laws that use language similar to IDEA. The differences between state and federal laws are generally in areas such as how each state defines disabilities or in the deadlines for completing evaluations to determine if a child is eligible for special education. The most important thing to know about state laws is that while they can provide additional rights and protections for students in special education, they cannot take away any rights and protections described in IDEA.

For example, our state's special education law has a more specific and enhanced definition of "effective progress" than IDEA.[7] This potentially adds additional protection for parents in any dispute with the school district about whether a student is receiving appropriate services and accommodations. Since all students in special education are required to receive the instruction and services they need to make effective progress, the additional clarity contained in the state law makes it easier to determine whether the services and accommodations are appropriate.

No Child Left Behind (NCLB)

The No Child Left Behind Act of 2001, while not primarily a special education law, does require that all students, including those with disabilities, be given "a fair, equal, and significant opportunity to obtain a high-quality education."[8] To achieve this, NCLB requires public schools receiving federal funding to give a yearly standardized test to all students. The test scores are supposed to indicate whether or not the school is meeting the standards set forth in the law. This makes the intent of NCLB somewhat incompatible with IDEA. Whereas NCLB is based on the principle of universal standards, IDEA is based on providing an individualized education. How this apparent incompatibility gets resolved is still a matter of debate as this book is being written.

SPECIAL EDUCATION FUNDING

When the original Education for All Handicapped Children Act was passed in 1975, Congress authorized the Federal Government to pay for 40 percent of all special education costs. Unfortunately, in the years that have followed, the government has managed to fund less than 20 percent of these costs. The latest estimates (2002–2003) from the U.S. Department of Education place the actual number at 17.1 percent.[9] The rest of the money to pay for special education comes from either the individual states or local communities. The amount of money contributed by each state varies widely as do the formulas for determining the reimbursement per student. This forces local school districts to make up whatever shortfall remains. This shortfall averages 47 percent of total special education funding nationwide according to a survey by the Center for Special Education Finance.[10]

Needless to say, reform of special education financing is a perennial topic of discussion in most state legislatures. States have tried a variety of solutions. Some states have a scale of funding that is determined by the type of disability. Others use "flat grant" funding, providing a fixed amount per student. Still other states fund special education based on the total school population in a district. After decades of trying different solutions, the lack of any consensus is indicative that every solution contains its own set of problems. No matter what formula states use, the intent of IDEA is that schools must meet the unique needs of the student regardless of the cost.

The special education business plan

The bottom line is that in most states almost half the burden for funding special education rests squarely on the individual school district and therefore on the local community. Yet, schools are expressly prohibited by IDEA from considering cost in deciding who is eligible for services and what those services should be.[11] The result is both a political and moral dilemma in which administrators have to balance budgets against need and yet not acknowledge that budget constraints even exist.

While it is easy to feel sympathy for the schools and administrators, the real losers are the students and their families, the most vulnerable and least powerful people in special education. For many school districts, special education becomes a calculated business. We believe that some school administrators have an unwritten business plan that is based on who will fight and who won't. Christopher Reeve, in his book *Nothing Is Impossible*, wrote about a parallel situation in the health care insurance industry. Reeve and his wife Dana discovered that "the main reason patients are routinely denied even the essentials [is that] only 30 percent fight back. Since 70 percent of their policyholders are easily intimidated, there is no upside for compliance."[12]

This was made clear to us during a public meeting of our town officials that we attended a few years ago. During the meeting a member of the town's finance committee asked the school superintendent questions about the proposed school budget for the coming year. Concerned that the town might be paying too much for special education services, the committee member wanted to know if students in special education were given only the services that the law required, or if they were given all the services parents asked for. The superintendent replied that at most the students received only what the law required, and to get even that much the parents were made to work for it.

With obstacles like these facing parents, we have observed that only a small percentage of them fight for their child's legal rights. The rest let the school district decide by default what defines an appropriate education for their child and even remain passive when schools deny services that are clearly indicated. Most parents don't have the time, the energy, or the resources to fight a denial of services. Many more don't even know that they have the right to do so. If parents do decide to fight for their child's rights, some school districts will pay large hourly fees to lawyers to fight back rather than put that money into needed services for students. Since schools in many parts of the country are funded with local fees or property taxes, they are, in essence, using the parents' own money to fight them. It is a lose/lose situation for families and the schools know it. The special education business plan has its own perverse logic.*

This situation isn't all the fault of educators. In fact, we have found that most people who go into special education do so out of a sincere desire to help the most vulnerable and needy in the student population. The problem comes when educators are required to do more and more with less and less due to lack of adequate funding. In our current economy, many extracurricular and academic activities in public schools now come with a fee attached. In some classrooms, even sheets of paper are considered an unessential "luxury" that shouldn't be provided at taxpayer expense.[14] As a result, the public school budget tends to limit special education services to a "one size fits all" approach that ultimately fits no one. In any political and economic climate it is hard to find support for special education. In difficult economic times, when educators may be tempted to conceal special education's shortcomings due to budget constraints and consistently overstate the progress made by special education students, the task may seem insurmountable.

THE FUTURE: PRIVATIZED SPECIAL EDUCATION?

A recent trend in special education is for public schools to hire outside contractors to administer their special education services. The incentive for school districts is, of course, saving money. A private company typically offers a fixed-cost contract to a school district at a rate that is less than whatever the district was paying for the same services on its own. While this outsourcing trend is too new to measure its effectiveness in the long run, an article in *Education Week* magazine profiling Futures Education LLC, "a private company that works with dozens of districts around the country on cutting special education costs," sheds some light on the possibilities.[15]

In the article, an interview with the company's CEO, Peter Bittel, reveals its approach: "The problem, according to Mr. Bittel, is that

---

* In 2012, one school district in Pennsylvania spent $329,084 defending itself against what was ultimately a $10,000 judgement.[13]

special education isn't standardized from school to school, much less across districts and states." In his view, schools offer too much therapy:

> Another example [Mr. Bittel] refers to often is providing therapy to teach children with disabilities to tie their shoes. "Is that educationally relevant?" Instead, he said, the child could wear shoes that don't need to be tied. He has the same attitude toward working for years to improve the handwriting of a child with disabilities. "Are we hurting the child? We'd argue we aren't," he said of putting aside that effort.

The CEO of Futures Education "argues" that not expecting a child to even try to learn to tie shoes or write by hand will ever hurt that child. It is hard to know where to begin with such an attitude. Our son had difficulty with fine motor skills, and in elementary school struggled with both tying his shoes and handwriting. Now that he is in his twenties, we can say with assurance that yes, it was very educationally relevant to address these deficits. Not to have done so would have hurt his chances for success as an adult. The same executive planning and fine motor skills needed to tie shoes or write legibly are needed to use a keyboard and drive a car. Not effectively addressing basic skills like these at the early stages simply increases a child's frustration at getting left behind. This, in turn, increases the need for psychological therapy in addition to the occupational therapy needed to address executive functioning and fine motor skills. Neglecting therapy now simply increases the need for therapy later and increases costs.

More concerning is Bittel's comment about a "standardized from school to school" approach for special education. IDEA is clear that special education services must support the whole child as an individual, not with "standardized," one-size-fits all services. How can Futures Education's goals be compatible with the letter, much less the spirit, of special education law?

In summary, the *Education Week* article quotes an assistant superintendent comparing his district's old special education services with the new, privatized ones, saying: "I don't think anyone would know the difference." If the standards promoted by Futures Education are indeed the future of special education, then it is hard not to view this statement as unintended irony.

FIGHTING THE LAST WAR

In trying to make sense of the current state of special education and project its future course, it is worth noting that special education laws have almost always addressed the problems of the past but have provided little guidance for the future, or arguably, even the present. The original Education for All Handicapped Children Act in 1975 addressed the problem of access to the mainstream classroom for students with physical or cognitive disabilities who had traditionally been excluded from any educational opportunities at all. It could not anticipate, however, the evolution in the understanding and diagnosis of learning disabilities that has occurred in the years since. For example, many children on the high functioning autism spectrum learn better in a classroom designed specifically for their unique learning style and heightened sensitivity to sensory stimuli. Yet a strict reading of even the most recent revision of IDEA still promotes the idea of inclusion in a classroom with predominantly neurotypical children, sparking endless debate between parents and school administrators about the meaning of "least restrictive environment." How that debate gets resolved can have a significant effect on the child in question.

In short, special education laws tend to be reactive rather than proactive. They primarily address a previous generation's understanding of special needs and learning disabilities, and not the reality with which most families dealing with special education must contend today. In this way, special education legislation is similar to the general who is prepared to fight the last war while being completely unprepared for the one he is about to face. If that sounds melodramatic, consider the lasting impact that an inadequate education can have. It can mean the difference between a dropout and a college graduate. We have seen multiple examples of both. In our experience, it is not the law that matters as much as the parents who make the effort to educate themselves about the complex process that is special education and have the willingness to apply that knowledge.

CHAPTER 1

GETTING STARTED IN SPECIAL EDUCATION

No parent approaches special education voluntarily. There is usually some event, behavior, diagnosis, or medical condition that sends parents to special education with concerns about their child. Having that first conversation with the director of special education is not a casual chat. We had that conversation when our son was three years old. Since he is now a young man and values his privacy, we will not disclose the details of that conversation in this book. But he has given us permission to write in general about his special needs and his school situation so that other families might benefit. In the following pages we will relate our family's experiences to the experience that other parents may have in dealing with special education.

This chapter describes the basic cycle of the special education process, from initial referral through the three-year reevaluation. This is a recurring cycle that will become familiar to parents with a child on an Individualized Education Program, or IEP. Understanding the special education cycle and knowing your rights and responsibilities within this cycle are key to making the special education experience work for the benefit of your child. This chapter also explains some of the basic concepts of the federal special education law, IDEA, that you will encounter.

AN OVERVIEW OF THE SPECIAL EDUCATION PROCESS

Special education is defined by IDEA as "specially designed instruction, at no cost to parents, to meet the unique needs of a child with a disability."[16] This instruction can be conducted in the classroom, in the home, in hospitals and institutions, and in other appropriate settings. The goal is to prepare students with disabilities for further education, employment, and independent living. Special education services provided by the public schools can begin at age three and continue through age 21,* or high school graduation, whichever comes first.

IDEA also outlines a specific process for determining eligibility for special education and, once eligibility is established, how services are given and progress is measured. The following is an overview of that process. Later chapters will expand on these brief explanations.

Referral

A parent, legal guardian, or teacher, and in some states other professionals who know the child, may request a referral to special education. Parents should send a written request for an initial eligibility evaluation to the special education department of their school district. The letter should describe the parent's or teacher's concerns about the child and the reasons why a referral is needed.† The school must then send the parent or guardian a consent form listing the types of evaluations that will be performed. Usually, the evaluations are selected with the parents' input. No evaluation can take place without a parent's written consent unless the school takes the parents to a due process hearing.

Evaluations

Once the school receives the signed consent form, it has 60 calendar days to complete the evaluations,[18] which have to cover all areas of suspected disabilities and must be performed by qualified and knowledgeable professionals. Initial evaluations should determine if a child has a qualifying disability under IDEA or applicable state laws. Most eligibility evaluations include educational assessments and psychological assessments. In addition, the school may perform evaluations in areas such as speech and language, occupational therapy, physical therapy, or adapted physical education as needed. Parents are entitled to review copies of all evaluations prior to the meeting that will discuss them. Although federal regulations do not specify how many days before a meeting parents are entitled to receive copies

---

* The age when special education services begin and end is left up to individual states. IDEA allows states to begin special education services between the ages of three and five and terminate these services between the ages of 18 and 21.[17]

† There are many sample referral letters available on the Internet that you can adapt for your own purposes. One good example can be found at: www.dredf.org/special_education/sampleletter-referra.pdf

of the evaluations, it does require that they be provided "without unnecessary delay."[19]

Eligibility meeting

Once the evaluations are complete, a Team composed of the parents and school specialists meets to discuss whether or not the tests show that a student is eligible for special education. There are established categories of disabilities that qualify for special education services, such as autism, developmental delay, or emotional, intellectual, neurological, and physical impairment. Specific disabilities in speech, writing, or the ability to do mathematical calculations also qualify for eligibility. Your state department of education's website will have a complete list.

In general, a student's disability must have a negative impact on his or her ability to make progress and access the general education curriculum in order to qualify for services. In some states, if a student needs a supportive service such as psychological counseling or physical therapy to access the general education curriculum, that alone is enough to qualify. At the meeting, parents should bring as much additional data as possible, such as letters from doctors or therapists, medical records, or reports of any outside testing that might reinforce their concerns and help the Team make its decision.

If the Team decides that a student is not eligible for special education, and the parents disagree, the parents can dispute this determination and can request an outside independent evaluation to support their belief that the student is eligible. See Chapter 3, "Outside Professionals," and Chapter 4, "Understanding School Evaluations," for information about independent evaluations and how to find professionals to perform them.

IEP meeting

Once the Team decides that a student is eligible for special education, it must write an IEP for that student. The Team will discuss the goals, services, and placement that will be included in this document. Unless the situation is unusually complex or the Team determines that eligibility is not warranted, the IEP meeting can be combined with the eligibility meeting. IDEA requires that a copy of the completed IEP be provided to parents within 60 days after the school receives the signed evaluation consent form. Parents must then accept or reject the completed IEP within a set time period that varies by state. Our state, for example, gives parents 30 days to accept or reject a completed IEP.

Goals and services

The IEP contains two important and related sections: 1) goals that the Team sets for the student to achieve during the period covered by the IEP, and 2) the services designed to help that student achieve those goals. Once both the parents and the school agree in writing to the goals and services, the school is legally obligated to provide the services listed starting on the date specified in the IEP.*

DIRECT, INDIRECT, AND RELATED SERVICES

All special education services provided to a student are based on the student's individual needs and are categorized as either direct, indirect, or related. Each category of services interacts with and supports the others. Knowing how this interaction will affect your child will help you make sure that your IEP has the appropriate mix of services.

- *Direct services* are those provided directly to a student in the classroom. These might include physical therapy or individual instruction in subjects like reading or math. In general, direct services are the ones that specifically support what a student is learning in school and may be provided in a regular education classroom or a separate special education classroom.

- *Indirect services* are those provided to the people who work with the student and enhance their ability to provide direct services. They could include training for the classroom teacher on how to teach students with disabilities, or consultation with an outside special education professional about a specific student's needs. Counseling services for parents to help them deal with the challenge of raising a child with special needs are also indirect services.

- *Related services* are those necessary for the student to benefit from the directly provided services. IDEA defines related

---

* For an IEP written in the late spring for the next school year, the services are usually scheduled to start at the beginning of the fall term. Otherwise, the date services begin should be the date the IEP is written and approved unless specifically stated otherwise.

services to include transportation as well as other supportive services such as speech and language therapy, psychological services, interpreting services, or physical and occupational therapy, among others. These services are often provided to the student in settings outside the classroom.

ACCOMMODATIONS AND MODIFICATIONS

Accommodations and modifications are two different approaches to providing special education services. Accommodations change the way instruction is provided or the way a student responds to it. An accommodation can be a different approach to the same assignment or test that students in regular education are working on. For instance, a student might have extra time on a test or seating in the front of the classroom as an accommodation. But he or she takes the same test as the rest of the class. Accommodations can also include the use of an assistive device, such as a specialized chair or desk, computer, or pencil grips.

Modifications change the educational program and can adjust the content of a test or assignment. This changes the expectations of the teacher and the standards of what a test or assignment will measure. An example might be a student with a math disability who is doing fifth-grade math in a seventh-grade math class. Or a student may be required to know half the words on a spelling test that the other students are learning. With modifications, the curriculum or the instruction can be changed for students with disabilities.

Both accommodations and modifications must be specified in a student's IEP.

Progress reports

Periodically, the school must send parents reports on whether or not their child is making effective progress toward his or her IEP goals. These reports have to be prepared at least as often as the school prepares grade reports for students in regular education. Usually that means quarterly progress reports.

Yearly review

Each year the student's Team must meet to assess the student's progress and make any necessary changes to the IEP. The Team should discuss the IEP goals and services and any other relevant issues. Parents or the school can also request a Team meeting at any time they feel one is necessary by submitting a request in writing.

Three-year reevaluation

Every three years the school must offer to reevaluate a student on an IEP to determine what the student's educational needs are at that time. If the parents and the school agree that a reevaluation is useful and necessary, the Team meets to discuss the results of the evaluations, including whether the student is still eligible for special education and, if so, how the new findings might affect the IEP.* Because it covers a longer time period than either the quarterly progress reports or the yearly IEP review meetings, the three-year reevaluation is one of the best chances that parents have to measure the progress their child is making and evaluate the goals and services he or she is receiving. This makes the three-year reevaluation as important as the initial evaluation meeting and, in a sense, marks the beginning of a new cycle in the special education process, with new goals, yearly IEP meetings, and progress reports.

ENTERING A COMPLEX AND LEGAL SITUATION

Once parents make the initial request for a special education referral and the special education cycle begins, parents enter into a new layer of bureaucracy and legal complexity. It is a world with its own rules and culture, and one for which few parents are prepared.

A family's first contact with their special education department after a referral request can be a confusing and stressful experience. To make this experience less confusing, you can request a preevaluation conference to talk with someone at your school about your child and discuss what evaluations will be performed. At this meeting, ask who will be performing the evaluations and what their credentials are. It is important that these people be qualified to perform the evaluations properly.

Our initial experience occurred when our son was three years old and was typical of how most parents enter into the process. For

---

* It is important to note that a school district cannot decide that a student is no longer eligible for special education services without performing a reevaluation.

us, getting the evaluations confirming our son's learning disabilities seemed like the end of a long search for answers. Our anxiety was relieved by the knowledge that we now had access to educational specialists trained to help our son. We reviewed his evaluations with members of our school district's special education staff. We all determined that he qualified for services and the Team agreed to write an IEP. Up to that point we had been feeling isolated and confused. Now we were part of a group effort and we started to relax, feeling we were in the hands of skilled professionals.

What we didn't understand was that special education is governed by specific laws that schools must follow. IDEA, as well as many states' regulations, exists to protect students and families in special education. We didn't know we had certain legal rights as well as obligations. We had no knowledge of IDEA or our state laws. We learned that in addition to understanding the overall process of special education, parents need to understand the basic concepts of IDEA. This starts with learning what the law means by "free appropriate public education," and "least restrictive environment," as well as the different interpretations that the law and subsequent court decisions apply to words like "inclusion" and "appropriate."

FAPE and LRE

Under IDEA there are two basic concepts: "free appropriate public education" (FAPE) and "least restrictive environment" (LRE). FAPE is what schools must provide for each student with a documented disability that qualifies them for special education. LRE refers to a student's placement in a school setting. These concepts are closely linked and one cannot be fully understood separately from the other.

IDEA addresses FAPE and LRE when it states that children with disabilities should be educated with children who are not disabled "[t]o the maximum extent appropriate," and that separate schools or classrooms should be used "only when the nature or severity of the disability of a child is such that education in regular classes with the use of supplementary aids and services cannot be achieved satisfactorily."[20] According to IDEA, the Team decides on a student's placement based solely on the evaluation data and an understanding of the placement options that meet the student's unique needs. Schools are not supposed to make placement decisions based on factors such as cost or administrative convenience.

The public school setting is the first placement option that the Team must consider as the LRE. This could be a general education classroom in the school that the student would normally attend. Within the classroom, the Team needs to decide what supplementary aids and services are sufficient to enable the student to make meaningful progress and benefit from interacting with non-disabled peers. But, if the general education classroom is not an appropriate placement, the question becomes how can LRE be applied "to the maximum extent appropriate."

A closer look at the law

Some school districts insist that they have no choice but to educate a student on an IEP in a general education classroom because that is always the least restrictive environment, and try to end the discussion there. This is not an accurate interpretation of the law, however, as court decisions have clearly stated that inclusion in a general education classroom should only be a secondary consideration when determining LRE for a student on an IEP.[21] If a student in special education cannot make meaningful progress studying in the same environment as students without disabilities, then the Team is required to offer different options, something IDEA refers to as a "continuum of alternative placements."[22] These placements could include specialized classes in a public school, a special education private school, home instruction, or even instruction in a hospital or institutional setting. In other words, LRE and a general education classroom are not automatically the same thing.

As one author has pointed out, the legal mandate of placing students in the least restrictive environment is supposed to protect students with disabilities, not "throw them into the deep end of the swimming pool before they have developed any of the requisite swimming skill sets."[23] Mainstreaming is not appropriate as the LRE if the nature or severity of a disability prevents the student from obtaining an appropriate education, regardless of how many supplementary aids and services are employed.

What is meant by "inclusion"?

Even when the LRE is the general education classroom, IDEA doesn't say how much time spent in that classroom (called "inclusion") is necessary. The answer, of course, depends on the individual student.

Spending the whole school day in a general education classroom (full inclusion) might be an appropriate placement for students with mild disabilities. For those with moderate to severe disabilities, full inclusion, even with many accommodations, could be a frustrating and ultimately damaging experience. So, the appropriate amount of inclusion is variable.

In our school district, which follows state guidelines, full inclusion is defined as services provided outside the general education classroom less than 21 percent of the time. In other words, the school provides no special education services outside the classroom during 80 percent of the student's school day. Partial inclusion means that special education services are provided outside the general education classroom at least 21 percent of the time but no more than 60 percent of the time.

A third option in a public school setting is a substantially separate classroom. In our district, this is defined as one where services are provided outside the general education classroom for more than 60 percent of the time. All other options involve placement outside of the public school, such as a special education day or residential school.

WHAT IS MEANT BY "APPROPRIATE"?

In IDEA, phrases such as "free appropriate education" and "to the maximum extent appropriate" appear often. The law does not say that students with special needs should have the best education; it says that they should have an education that fits the individual needs of the student and allows the student to make educational progress. The questions that often divide parents and school administrators are how broadly to interpret what is meant by "appropriate" and how to measure a student's progress.

We have encountered school administrators who wanted us to believe that special education is only concerned with what is appropriate academically. In fact, IDEA requires that in addition to academic needs, school districts must address a student's unique social and emotional needs if they impact the student's ability to learn. Unfortunately, IDEA leaves it up to each state to define how academic progress is measured. In Maryland, for example, lack of progress occurs "when an individual's appropriate levels of effort do not result in reasonable progress given the opportunity for effective education instruction." Maryland law further states that progress, or lack of progress, "cannot be determined solely by a quantitative test score."[24] This statute acknowledges that progress is not simply a matter of acquiring knowledge, but includes emotional growth and appropriate social integration in the classroom. In other words, how your state chooses to define "inclusion" and "appropriate," and how it measures progress can have a significant effect on what services and instruction your child receives. This makes it critical that you make an effort to determine your particular state's definition of these terms.

WHAT PARENTS CAN DO

It's one thing to read about special education laws and procedures and another to translate that knowledge into action. At the end of each chapter we offer a list of suggestions on how you can use the information in that chapter.

- If you suspect your child has a learning disability and are considering asking for a referral to special education, look at data such as your child's grades, behavior, and classroom observations for clues. Ask yourself if the data shows that your child is performing at grade level and benefiting from his or her education. The more objective information that you can collect and share, the more likely it will be that evaluations will accurately present a picture of your child's specific needs.

- The school must perform evaluations in all suspected areas of disability, but you have to consent to these evaluations in writing before the school can do them. When you get the consent form, read it carefully before you sign. If there are sections that aren't clear to you, such as the purpose of the recommended evaluations or the credentials of the evaluators, ask for a telephone conversation or a meeting with the special education coordinator of your school to discuss your concerns. If you believe that evaluations in additional areas are necessary, you can request them. After you return the signed consent form, follow through with the school staff to make sure that all the evaluations are actually performed.

- You are entitled to see copies of all evaluations prior to any Team meeting that will discuss them, and the school is obligated to provide them "without unnecessary delay and before any meeting regarding an IEP." You should make this request in writing (see Chapter 9, "The Paper Trail," for reasons why such requests should always be in writing). It is important to read these evaluations ahead of time and be prepared to discuss them at the meeting. If you do not get the reports within a reasonable time before the meeting, consider postponing the meeting until you have adequate time for review. We have had school evaluations that were based on inaccurate data delivered on the morning of a scheduled meeting. The result was a wasted meeting that had to be repeated two weeks later.

• Request an outside independent evaluation as a "second opinion" if you disagree with the Team's decision about your child's eligibility for special education. You may have to pay for the evaluation yourself, though it is possible to have the school pay for it under certain circumstances. See Chapter 3, "Outside Professionals," and Chapter 4, "Understanding School Evaluations," for more information about when to consider an independent evaluation and who should perform it.

• When you discuss placement options with your IEP Team, be sure to ask about what "continuum of alternative placements" are available. The least restrictive environment that can meet your child's needs is not always the regular education classroom, even with supplementary aids and services. Be aware that regular education teachers may not have training in educating students with special needs.*

• If you have concerns regarding your child or the services he or she is receiving, you can request a Team meeting to discuss these concerns. You do not have to wait for the yearly IEP review meeting before these issues get addressed. The Team can convene to make changes to the IEP at any time as the need arises.

• If your school wants to terminate special education services, it must reevaluate your child and provide objective data that prove your child no longer qualifies for these services in every area in which he or she did qualify previously. Simply saying that a student is making effective progress through classroom performance is not enough.

---

*   A survey conducted by *Education Week* magazine discovered that only 14 states and the District of Columbia required regular education teachers to complete one or more courses in special education subjects.[25]

- Find an online source of the laws that apply to special education in your particular state that you can search if you have questions. The department of education in every state we have researched maintains a website that contains links to these laws. While IDEA's provisions apply in all situations, you may find that in certain areas, your state grants additional rights that are worth knowing about.

- Realize that you have begun a journey that will test your patience and perseverance. The special education experience is composed of many complex and sometimes contradictory parts. These include state and federal laws, unwritten school rules, an unfamiliar bureaucratic culture, and the emotional impact of coping with your child's disability. Your motivation should always be to help your child succeed in school, academically, emotionally, and socially.

CHAPTER 2

SCHOOL PERSONNEL

There are many professionals who may interact with you and your child in a public school setting. You will encounter these individuals on both the regular education staff and the special education staff. If you understand their roles and how they fit within the structure of the school setting you will know who controls the decisions in special education that affect you and your child. This chapter reviews the different personnel you will likely encounter and their functions.

ADMINISTRATION

There is a hierarchy in public schools with the superintendent at the top. He or she is the most powerful person in the district. Other school personnel with whom you are more likely to interact cannot make major decisions without the ultimate approval of the superintendent. Even in areas where special education personnel have discretion, they are unlikely to make decisions outside the framework of school policy determined by the superintendent. Ultimately, this person is responsible only to the town's School Committee, which hires and supervises the superintendent.

Below the superintendent are many administrative personnel, including the assistant superintendent, the business administrator, the director of special education, the out-of-district coordinator for special education, and the early childhood specialist, if the district has one. There can be other positions as well, such as directors of transportation and the before- and after-school programs. The job of the administration is to set policy and supervise all the schools in the district.

The top administrative person in each school is the principal. Sometimes there are assistant principals as well as administrative staff in the school's office, such as secretaries, who are essential to the efficient running of the school.

REGULAR EDUCATION PROFESSIONALS

Regular education professionals provide the general education that most students receive. Parents are likely to be familiar with their child's classroom teachers, but in addition, there are many other regular education professionals who work with students during the school day. These include physical education teachers, librarians, and specialists in art and music.

Classroom teachers

The No Child Left Behind Act of 2001 (NCLB) requires that school districts hire highly qualified teachers to teach academic core subjects, such as English, mathematics, reading and language arts, history, science, and foreign languages.[26] These teachers must have at least a Bachelor's degree as well as full state certification or licensure. They must satisfy requirements for demonstrating competence in their subject areas. Your state's department of education website will list the specific requirements.

In a typical elementary school setting, students are with one regular education teacher all day in a class of about 20 to 25 students. There might be an assistant regular education teacher or a special education teacher in the classroom as well. Students on IEPs are sometimes part of small groups within the regular education classroom for more specific instruction, or they might have one-on-one instruction in a resource room with a special education teacher or paraprofessional. They might also be fully integrated into a mainstream classroom setting with help from a special education teacher or aide.

In a typical middle school or high school setting, students have multiple teachers throughout the school day as they move from classroom to classroom. Since regular education teachers might have 80 or more students a day to teach, most can give only limited personal attention to a student on an IEP. Students who need extra help are usually given a class period in a resource room where a special education teacher works with them.

Physical education teachers, librarians, art and music specialists

In addition to classroom teachers, there are also many regular education specialists who interact with students. There are art and music teachers as well as physical education teachers and librarians. If a student has a special need that limits his or her participation, the IEP should specify appropriate services, including an aide, so the student can access the curriculum in these areas.

Guidance counselors

School guidance counselors perform many functions for both regular education and special education students that typically vary according to grade level. In elementary school, a guidance counselor might concentrate on helping students develop study or social skills, either through individual or group counseling, and confer with teachers and parents about a student's strengths and weaknesses. In middle school and high school, guidance counselors might spend more time with students to develop academic and career goals. By the time a student approaches graduation, the guidance counselor will advise students about college or vocational choices.

SPECIAL EDUCATION PROFESSIONALS

The role of special education professionals is to provide services that are customized to meet a student's unique needs. They can provide specialized instruction both within the general education classroom and in separate learning environments, as well as assess a student's strengths and weaknesses through evaluations, write IEPs, and attend Team meetings. The following are descriptions of the most common special education professionals you will encounter:

Liaisons

Most students on an IEP have a special education teacher who acts as a liaison with the parents. It is the liaison who is in charge of developing the IEP and seeing that its goals are implemented. Of all the special education professionals in the school, parents generally work most closely with a liaison who serves as their contact with the other specialists, as well as with the school's overall special education program.

In addition to serving as facilitators and administrators, some elementary school liaisons assist regular education teachers in the classroom by focusing on the students who are on IEPs. The liaison can also pull students out of the classroom for specialized instruction. The location where they work with their students is commonly referred to as a "resource room," which is usually a quiet area where students can receive one-on-one or small group instruction. In middle school or high school, most of the interaction between liaisons and their students occurs in the resource room.

Paraprofessionals, aides, and teaching assistants

Schools often hire additional people to help teachers with special education students. A paraprofessional, aide, or teaching assistant can be with a student part of the day or all day to provide instruction under the direction of a classroom teacher. Other duties can include working on clerical tasks, communicating with parents, or supervising children in the cafeteria, hallways, playgrounds, and on field trips. Salaries can be low for these positions, which are often part-time with few or no benefits. States have different minimum requirements for aides and teaching assistants, usually a high school diploma or an associate's degree from a community college. Check with your state department of education to get more information on what requirements are necessary for these positions in your area.

Paraprofessionals have a different status under the federal NCLB mandate. NCLB defines "paraprofessional" and the necessary education and certification requirements that person must have to work with special education students. The titles "aide" and "teaching assistant" are not defined by the law and therefore do not require the same qualifications. Some schools will use the words aide, paraprofessional, and teaching assistant interchangeably, when in fact paraprofessionals are held to higher standards than aides or teaching assistants, who can lack the necessary background to work with students who have disabilities.

RELATED SERVICE PROVIDERS

In addition to the special education professionals who work within the general education curriculum, there are a number of professionals who provide specialized services to students with disabilities. The list of these providers is as varied as the special needs they work with, and includes remedial reading instructors, instructors for the visually impaired, mobility specialists, and teachers of the deaf and hard of hearing. The following descriptions include the related service providers we encountered who most often work with students in special education:

Psychologists

Psychologists are an important part of the general education staff, as they provide services to students, families, teachers, and administrators in a variety of roles. School psychologists can help students who are afraid to go to school, who are depressed or anxious, who need help with study skills, who are failing courses, or who are having other difficulties. They collaborate with other professionals within the school and can coordinate resources outside the school to help a student. In general, school psychologists work to create a positive classroom and school environment, and implement mental health services for all students.

In special education, school psychologists play a critical role since they can perform evaluations to test for learning problems, identify strengths and weaknesses, and interpret test results. The school psychologist can also discuss recommendations with a student's teachers to create a supportive learning environment and develop appropriate interventions if any are needed.

Qualifications for a school psychologist should include training in both the fields of psychology and education. Most districts require an advanced degree in school psychology as well as a passing score on state or national certified exams. School psychologists must also have the proper certification for the state in which they work. In addition, certification by the National School Psychology Certification Board and the National Association of School Psychologists insures high standards and ethical behavior.

Generally, school psychologists and guidance counselors perform different functions, but there can be overlap. In our school district, there were licensed psychologists working as guidance counselors, and in at least one instance, a certified guidance counselor working as a school psychologist. Their functions seemed interchangeable.

Speech and language pathologists

Speech and language pathologists work with students who have difficulty with various types of communication, such as pronouncing sounds and problems with processing or producing spoken or written language. Speech and language disorders can affect reading, writing, speaking, and listening, all necessary skills in school. These professionals can also help with language pragmatics such as speaking volume control, eye contact, appropriate distance between people, and initiating, maintaining, and terminating a conversation. Speech and language pathologists can even help students who have difficulty swallowing pills, a common problem for children with sensory difficulties.

Occupational therapists

Occupational therapists work with people to improve their ability to perform the activities of daily living or "occupations." Reasons for needing occupational therapy include injury, illness, developmental delays, and learning disabilities. In a school setting, occupational therapists work with students in academic and non-academic areas so they can be successful in all aspects of the school day.

Occupational therapy helps students with fine and gross motor skills, which can improve their experiences on the playground and in the classroom. They also work on motor planning, so that a student can understand a logical sequence to begin and end a task. In addition, occupational therapists help students who are overly sensitive to external stimuli by integrating the sounds and activities of daily life into their routines. These therapists use exercises to help students process sensory information and help them develop their abilities to play and ultimately to learn.

Many schools have only limited occupational therapy resources. Working with gross motor skills can require a significant amount of room and specialized equipment. In elementary school, our son mostly received occupational therapy for fine motor skills, such as holding a pencil and working on his handwriting. We employed an outside occupational therapy clinic to provide additional sensory integration therapy for gross motor skills. In Chapter 3, "Outside Professionals," we have more information on when to consider using private professionals and how to find them.

Physical therapists

Physical therapists, like occupational therapists, help children achieve their educational goals by improving the quality of movement and function in a school setting. Some of the areas that a physical therapist might address are muscle strength, range of motion, sensory processing, mobility, and endurance. A physical therapist can assess movement and physical requirements for various school activities like navigating a hallway, staircase, bathroom, classroom, cafeteria, or playground, and help students who have difficulty with walking, balance, or posture. This professional can also advise parents and teachers on the need for equipment such as wheelchairs or modified desks and chairs for students who require this kind of adaptation.

Adapted physical education instructors

Because physical education is required for students in 41 states, schools in these states must provide appropriate alternative activities when a student is unable to participate in a regular physical education program. Adapted Physical Education (APE) is physical education adapted to include students who would struggle with a more mainstream physical education program. An APE instructor might employ special activities, equipment, or a different environment as an alternative to the standard curriculum.

In addition to motor planning or motor skill difficulties, some students also need help with social behavior in a gym setting. An APE instructor can also involve students who are not on IEPs in an activity with students on IEPs. This helps students with disabilities learn to socialize as well as providing them with the necessary motor planning and physical skills.

PROPER CREDENTIALS

It is possible for some professionals to work in a school system many years without the proper credentials for their job. Others may be working under a waiver or with a provisional status, indicating that they may not yet have the appropriate educational background or experience to obtain full department of education certification. All states require special education professionals to meet certain minimum requirements for certification, which include at least a Bachelor's degree. These requirements should be listed on your state's Department of Education website.*

State professional licenses (outside of department of education certification) for certain professions, like speech and language pathologists, social workers, and psychologists, are not always required in a school setting but provide an indication of someone's standing in their profession and, more importantly, can serve as a protection for parents. If there is a problem with a licensed professional and you feel the professional has not behaved properly, you can file a complaint with the state licensure board and they will investigate. A professional without a license is not accountable to a licensure board. Also be aware that the reason a professional does not have a license may be that he or she does not have sufficient educational credentials to obtain a license or that he or she might have failed a background check. The U.S. Department of Education has estimated that 13 percent of jobs in special education were either vacant or filled by someone without proper credentials.[27]

Checking credentials: A case study

While many special education professionals are properly certified for the students they work with, do not assume that all specialists working in your school system have the correct credentials. Special education professionals are only required to be "highly qualified" by NCLB if they are instructing students in a core subject. We discovered that two important professionals working with students in our district's high school were lacking the proper department of education certification to do their jobs even though they were longtime employees, in one case for over a decade. We realized this when our school wanted to place our son in a program for special education students when he started high school. We began researching the credentials of the school psychologist, who was an important part of this program. We learned that, even though he did have an advanced degree, he was not licensed by the state to practice psychology. Even more disturbing, he was not certified by the department of education as a school psychologist. His only certification was as a guidance counselor for students up to the

---

* The Education Commission of the States has a useful web page: "Special Education Teacher Certification and Licensure" that allows you to select a state and the type of certification/ licensure, for example general education or special education, and it will show you the requirements for that state. http://mb2.ecs.org/reports/reporttq.aspx?id=1542&map=0

ninth grade. Yet, he was prominently listed in the school handbook as the high school's only psychologist, working with students through grade 12.

Digging a little deeper, we contacted professional organizations, such as the National Association of School Psychologists. School psychologists in our state must meet the qualification standards of this organization as one requirement for certification as a school psychologist. We also contacted the National Board for Certified Counselors, which likewise has qualification standards that our state requires for certification as a school guidance counselor. None of the organizations we contacted had heard of him. While it is legal in our state for a psychologist to work in a public school without a professional license, not having the proper department of education certification is not.

After discovering that the school psychologist lacked proper credentials, we then found out that the director of the same high school program was also lacking proper certification for her position. These discoveries had a significant bearing on our decision to seek placement for our son at a private special education school that was better prepared to teach him.

SPECIAL EDUCATION ETIQUETTE

Special education can be both rewarding for parents and a source of frustration when things don't go the way they should. While some experts believe that conflict between parents and schools is normal and inevitable,[28] it is too easy to become frustrated with the special education system and take it out on the individuals in the system you encounter most often. For the most part, it would be unfair to confuse the individual with the system. Teachers and other professionals who choose special education as a vocation usually do so out of a genuine interest in helping students and can be as frustrated by the system as parents. Whenever you are tempted to display your anger and frustration, our best advice (paraphrasing investor Warren Buffet), is to remember these two rules:

1. The special education experience is not about you, it is about your child.

2. Never forget rule number one.

What we mean by this is that no matter how many violations of the special education law the school commits and no matter how angry that makes you, do not take the situation personally. Always do your best to maintain a cordial relationship with the people who are teaching your child, providing services to your child, or administering the program your child attends. You need their help for your son or daughter to get an appropriate education. Confrontation only makes school personnel defensive and less cooperative. To quote one expert: "Unless you are prepared to remove your child from public school forever, you need to view your relationship with the school as a marriage without the possibility of divorce."[29]

If necessary, you can seek remedies for problems in a due process hearing (see Chapter 10, "The Legal Process"), but if you do, the hearing officer will want to know that you first have made every effort to cooperate and try reasonable suggestions that school personnel offer. It is fine to point out problems and seek to negotiate solutions, but if you go to a hearing with a history of confrontation and lack of cooperation, that will inevitability be factored into any judgement the hearing officer makes. In short, there is no downside to being polite, even if you feel that the courtesy is not reciprocal. To that end, we have the following suggestions to help you maintain an appropriate relationship with school personnel:

- Treat the people working with your child as you would like to be treated. What you perceive as lack of cooperation may be the result of being overwhelmed by having to work with too many students or being hamstrung by lack of resources, rather than an intentional slight. It doesn't help to be rude or dismissive of people who are doing their best in less than ideal circumstances.

- Don't assume that school personnel understand all the details of your child's disability. Be willing to spend some time educating Team members about your child's particular needs. Sometimes parents mistake a lack of understanding as a lack of cooperation.

- Prioritize what is most important for your child's education and do not make a habit of complaining about small procedural errors or trying to control all the details of your child's school life. Save your energy and credibility for the important problems. Ask yourself if you would rather be angry or get appropriate services for your child.

- Find a forum other than a Team meeting to express anger or frustration. Use a spouse or trusted friend for animated discussions about things you feel the school is not doing appropriately. A trained advocate can be a good sounding board for your concerns as well as a source of advice for how to proceed when you encounter roadblocks. See Chapter 3, "Outside Professionals," for information on finding and working with a special education advocate.

- Keep an open mind at Team meetings and consider all suggestions thoughtfully, even ones with which you might disagree. If you find a discussion over a disagreement becoming too heated, or if a Team member starts to lose emotional control, ask for a short break or, if necessary, ask that the meeting be reconvened at a later date.

- Even if your school is not following the letter of the special education laws, your job is to insure that your child gets the help he or she needs, not to point out the school's failures, or worse, try to get the school to admit its failures. School districts, like all bureaucracies, will hardly ever do that. To this end, concentrate on the solutions to problems, not on the failure that might have caused the problem.

None of this means that you have to accept improper behavior from school personnel or not stand up for the rights of your child. Your ultimate goal is to create a positive working environment in which you can advocate for your child and negotiate for appropriate services and supports.

WHAT PARENTS CAN DO

Here is a list of suggestions on how you can use the information in this chapter:

- Notice the title of any person providing services to your child if it is other than the classroom teacher or liaison. Paraprofessionals are required by federal law to have specific qualifications, but aides and teaching assistants are not. If the service that an aide or teaching assistant is providing is complicated or involves technical knowledge, then ask that a qualified paraprofessional work with your child. You may also want to ask about the supervision that the paraprofessional, aide, or teaching assistant is receiving.

- Be aware that speech and language pathologists can diagnose problems and provide services in many areas beyond obvious speech difficulties. If you have a speech and language evaluation performed by the school that does not address issues such as language pragmatics or executive functioning and you feel these services are needed, question it. If the school will not test in these areas and you feel that they are needed, you may have to get an outside evaluation performed. See Chapter 3, "Outside Professionals," for information on finding an outside professional to perform an evaluation.

- Make sure that your child will receive appropriate instruction or support if he or she has a class period in a middle school or high school resource room. This time should not be just an unstructured study hall.

- Be sure that your child's IEP includes physical education services that are appropriate to his or her needs. This may require a qualified adapted physical education teacher.

- Check the credentials of important staff members who will be working with your child. Certification of teachers and support staff is a matter of public record. You have a right to know a teacher's or staff person's educational degrees, whether that person has met the appropriate qualification and licensing criteria, and whether he or she is working with a licensing waiver or under a provisional status. There are a number of sample letters available on the Internet that you can use as starting points for making a written request, such as: www.wrightslaw.com/info/nclb.ltr.teacher.qual.pdf. For state licenses, most states have a Division of Professional Licensure website where you can search for an individual's license status. Otherwise, you can call or write your state's licensure board inquiring about the status of an individual's license.

- Always try to be cooperative and polite when working with school employees and appreciate what they can do for your child. Try to follow the "special education etiquette" described in this chapter and realize that there are more effective ways to advocate for appropriate services than being confrontational with the people who work most directly with your child.

CHAPTER 3

OUTSIDE PROFESSIONALS

Sometimes, schools can't do all the tests needed to accurately evaluate and understand your child's disability. Other times, they can't offer the right therapies in enough depth, frequency, or duration to benefit your child. Or, you might disagree with school professionals about what services your child needs. When you encounter one or more of these situations, it limits your ability to know the extent of your child's needs and how to meet them. This is a time to consider seeking an independent professional who can give you an unbiased evaluation, administer more in-depth therapy, or help you advocate for more appropriate services. This chapter tells you when to consult an outside professional, how to find the right one, and describes the most common types of independent professionals you might need.

WHEN DO YOU NEED AN OUTSIDE PROFESSIONAL?

You may want to work with an outside professional for a variety of reasons that depend on your child's disabilities, the services the school is offering (or not offering), and the changing landscape of special education laws and regulations. The following examples illustrate some possible reasons:

- If your child's disability is significant or complex, the school may not have a properly qualified person with the training needed to make a fully detailed evaluation. An independent specialist with the proper knowledge can make an in-depth evaluation and diagnosis of your child with specific recommendations for your child's school program.

- While schools usually offer many services and different types of therapies, they may lack the space, specialized equipment, or trained staff to provide all that your child might need. Outside professionals in a setting specifically designed for a particular type of therapy can supplement what your school can offer.

- You might feel that your school is minimizing your child's needs and is recommending inadequate or even no services. Rather than wonder whether or not your concerns are valid, or try to negotiate with the special education administrators of your school district by yourself, you can seek the help of a special education advocate. The advocate can review the available testing data and help you interpret it, recommend additional independent evaluations if necessary, and accompany you to Team meetings. An advocate can also help you decide when you may need the help of a special education lawyer.

FINDING PROFESSIONALS

It is easier to find a suitable professional if you start in the right place. The Parent Technical Assistance Center Network website (www.parentcenternetwork.org) has a convenient tool for locating the parent center in your state. These centers can give you referrals to local professionals. The Yellow Pages for Kids with Disabilities (www.yellowpagesforkids.com) contains information on evaluators, tutors, advocates, therapists, and many more, grouped by state. Another nationwide organization that provides referrals and support for parents is the Learning Disabilities Association of America (www.ldanatl.org).

You should also investigate your area's support groups for parents of children with special needs. Our state requires each school district to have a Special Education Parent Advisory Council, or SEPAC, run by parent volunteers. Contact your director of special education to see if there is a similar organization in your district. Attend meetings and ask other parents if they can recommend appropriate professionals.

Once you locate a professional you are interested in, call that person and ask questions about his or her credentials. If you are seeking an outside evaluation, ask about the kind of testing the professional does, how long it takes, and what kind of report you can expect. Be sure to check on this person's background, experience, and membership in professional associations, as well as academic degrees. Also check on the fees and payment schedule, because some therapies and evaluations can be costly and may not be fully covered by insurance.* During your first interview, describe your child's problems and listen carefully to that person's responses. Try to get a sense of his or her style and personality and whether or not you feel comfortable with that person. Finally, ask for references and talk to other parents who have used this professional. Ask if the kind of information you are seeking is similar to what they were looking for.

Most importantly, ask if the professional is willing to come to a Team meeting, or if he or she would be willing to testify on your child's behalf at a due process hearing, should that become necessary. A complex report such as a neuropsychological evaluation, even if it is an excellent one, is not as convincing as the presence of the person who wrote it and who can explain the details to the Team or a hearing officer. Knowing that a professional is willing to do this indicates how helpful that professional is likely to be. It also might reveal if that person has any financial or other relationship with your school district that could affect how he or she will advocate for your child. Consider that something as simple as whether or not the professional has a child currently attending a school in your district might make that person less willing to stand up to the school in advocating on your child's behalf. There is more detail about this issue in Chapter 5, "Conflicts of Interest."

WHEN IS A PROFESSIONAL RIGHT FOR YOUR CHILD?

Be aware that not every professional is right for you and your child. We hired a reading tutor for our son when he was in first grade. We had attended a lecture she gave, liked her presentation, and had gotten a recommendation from another parent in our town. But at our son's first appointment, we overheard this tutor berating him about his inability to read instead of encouraging him. We were incredulous that she would talk to a young child this way. We never made a second appointment.

Similarly, over the years we encountered three different psychologists who simply did not know how to deal with our son's learning disabilities, despite assurances that they had a great deal of experience in the area. Their advice was not only inadequate, but

---

* There are certain situations in which the school must pay for an outside evaluation. See the section "Independent Educational Evaluations" in Chapter 4, "Understanding School Evaluations," for more information.

sometimes wrong, and our experience with them cost us valuable time, especially when our son needed help in middle school. Other parents have told us that their child's therapist simply blamed them for their child's problems.

When you encounter a professional who is not right for you and your child, terminate the relationship and find someone else. Even after getting recommendations and doing a lot of research and interviewing, we still encountered a few professionals we had to leave. In some cases, it was just the wrong fit; in others there was obvious incompetence. Conversely, we also found many excellent professionals who made a real difference for us and our son. Value these people and try to stay with them.

Ultimately, trust your feelings about a professional. Even though you may not have the credentials that this person has, you are the one who knows your child better than anyone else. If an evaluation doesn't seem to describe the child you know, or if you don't see the progress you feel your child should be making in a therapy or tutoring session, question it. If the answer doesn't reassure you, go elsewhere. Remember, you are building a team of experts on whom you will be relying for many years.

PROFESSIONALS TO CONSIDER

There are a wide variety of professionals you might need to consult, depending on your child's needs. There are medical professionals for physical and mental issues, therapists who are trained to assist with specific disabilities, educational professionals who can evaluate school programs, and finally, people who provide advocacy and legal services. In some cases, there is overlap in the services these professionals provide. The following are descriptions of some of the most common professionals that you might want to consider:

Medical specialists

Asking your child's pediatrician about medical or behavioral concerns is always a good place to start. For complex or significant special needs, you should get a referral to a medical specialist who has more expertise in a specific area. Your pediatrician should be able to help you find the right one.

Mental health professionals

There are at least three different types of mental health professionals you can consult, depending on the type of services you need: social workers, psychologists, and psychiatrists. Social workers can work with families regarding behavioral problems, family dynamics, or emotional issues. Psychologists can do this as well and also perform many types of educational and psychological testing. A psychiatrist may be the best choice for an assessment of complex emotional issues or treatment that might involve medication.

Speech and language pathologists

Speech and language pathologists assess how a child understands and uses language. Specifically, they can evaluate and treat how a child uses spoken language, receptive language, written language, and pragmatic language. They can treat a wide range of disorders, such as speech sound disorders (how a child pronounces words), language disorders (how a child understands and expresses words), stuttering, voice disorders (quality of the voice and volume), and others.

Occupational therapists

Occupational therapists help students with their daily activities so that they can succeed in school. The treatment they offer depends on a student's needs. For example, if a student has poor fine motor skills, an occupational therapist can work on holding a pencil correctly to improve handwriting or learning to tie shoelaces. There are many exercises that an occupational therapist can recommend for students to improve school skills.

While many districts have one or more occupational therapists on staff, some schools have limits on how much time and specialized equipment they can devote to occupational therapy. If your child needs more intensive services with different kinds of equipment, you may have to find a clinic that specializes in occupational therapy. This kind of clinic will probably have more expertise, space, and equipment to help your child than your school has.

Adapted physical education instructors

Adapted physical education (APE) teachers work with students on gross motor skills and coordination in a gym class that has been modified, or "adapted," to meet the student's needs. Although this is a service that most schools provide for students, this is also an area where schools may have limited resources and facilities. Independent providers who offer this kind of physical education class typically have a larger space, more equipment, and more staff. Like occupational therapy, this can be a good therapy to supplement outside the school setting.

Special needs horseback riding instructors

Horseback riding can be beneficial for many students with a variety of special needs. The benefits of this type of therapy include improvements in fine motor coordination, muscle tone, strength, posture, spatial awareness, and balance. Another name for this therapy is hippotherapy, derived from the Greek word "hippos" for horse.

The American Hippotherapy Association (www.americanhippo therapyassociation.org) has information on finding instructors and facilities. Hippotherapy instructors can be occupational therapists, physical therapists, or speech and language pathologists who use the horse's gait to provide sensory input to clients. Equine movement, combined with exercises directed by the therapist, can help with many special needs and impairments.

Neuropsychologists

A neuropsychologist typically has a doctorate in psychology and specializes in how the brain functions. This professional can diagnose and assess many learning disabilities, such as deficits in abstract reasoning, memory skills, motor skills, executive functioning, and attention. A neuropsychologist can also diagnose certain emotional and other psychological disorders. A neuropsychological evaluation can provide a comprehensive picture of how your child learns, including detailed information on strengths and weaknesses. Some practices offering this kind of testing also offer additional resources, such as social skills groups and tutoring.

A neuropsychological report is the most comprehensive evaluation of a student available, for it explains how a child learns and functions.

It is a key document to help parents fully understand their child's disability and provide evidence to help parents secure appropriate services for their child at school. An independent neuropsychologist is also an excellent professional to attend Team meetings, observe a child's program, or go to special education hearings to explain the needs of a child in an educational setting.

Before you decide on neuropsychological testing, explain to the doctor that you are looking for a report with understandable, specific recommendations that can be written into your child's IEP and effectively implemented by the school. One neuropsychologist we consulted gave us a report that was highly technical and did not fully explain important details or give clear recommendations. As a result, we missed asking for some key services in our son's elementary and middle school IEPs.

Try to do a neuropsychological evaluation every three years or so, as it will give you a more complete picture of who your child is and how his or her strengths and weaknesses change over time. If your child is planning to go to college, a recent neuropsychological evaluation is especially important, because testing organizations such as the College Board require this type of evidence before they will allow accommodations on entrance exams such as the SAT or ACT. In addition, colleges want up-to-date testing before they will provide accommodations to students who disclose their special needs to the school's disability support staff.

Educational consultants

An educational consultant can evaluate how a student learns, observe current and proposed placements for students, and recommend what kind of placement is appropriate. This professional can be very helpful if you need advice and recommendations about your child's overall educational experience. It is important to choose a consultant who understands special education and your child's particular disability. If a dispute arises over a student's placement, a consultant can visit the current school setting and the proposed school setting to observe and make recommendations. An educational consultant is a good choice to attend Team meetings and even hearings to discuss what a student needs in a school setting.

Advocates

Parents with children on IEPs should consider using the services of a trained advocate if they need help understanding their child's needs or navigating the special education system. It can be emotionally difficult for parents to realistically face the problems of a child with disabilities. When you add managing a child's documents, understanding special education laws, and making sure a child is receiving appropriate services, a good advocate can be indispensable.

Even when you read your child's IEP carefully, you may not fully understand all the implications of what you are reading. An advocate can help you evaluate an IEP and understand how well your child is doing toward fulfilling the IEP goals. Even more important, an advocate can attend Team meetings with you to discuss services and make sure that the services are adequate. If there is a single outside professional you should consider above all others, it is an advocate. Such a person can ultimately save you time and money, as well as frustration.

In some states special education advocates specialize in either legal or educational advocacy. A legal advocate, often referred to as a "lay advocate," is not a lawyer, but has specialized training in legal matters that pertain to special education. Lay advocates can attend Team meetings, write letters, and negotiate with schools to help resolve problems. In some states they can even represent parents in due process hearings. Educational advocates specialize in helping evaluate various disabilities and making recommendations about accommodations and services. In general, there can be a lot of overlap between the functions of lay and educational advocates.

Look for an advocate who has received appropriate training and knows the special education laws. In Massachusetts, a group called the Federation for Children with Special Needs provides a program that trains special needs advocates. See if there is a reputable group in your area that offers training and might be able to refer you to someone who has completed this training with them. This is essential, since currently there are no licensing requirements for advocates. The best advocates are ones who know the laws, understand your child's disability, and have experience working cooperatively with school districts. Some state departments of education provide useful information on how to select a special education advocate on their websites.

Once you have hired an advocate, share your school and independent evaluations with this person. An experienced advocate can read these reports more objectively than you and should be able to advise you on whether or not the recommendations are appropriate. The advocate can also attend Team meetings to discuss recommendations in school reports and the reports of outside professionals. The ultimate goal for an advocate is to help parents understand special education and empower them to make informed decisions for their child.

Finally, if you feel that your child is not receiving appropriate services, if you have worked with an advocate and the situation is still not resolved, it may be time to consider hiring an attorney. If it comes to that, then an advocate should be able to help you gather and organize the necessary documentation to present your case before you start paying a lawyer's billable hours. This can ultimately save you money and make your case stronger. Finding a lawyer and pursuing your legal rights is the subject of Chapter 10, "The Legal Process."

WHAT PARENTS CAN DO

Here is a list of suggestions on how you can use the information in this chapter:

- Be proactive about seeking an outside professional if you see a problem developing. Do not passively "wait and see" if the problem will disappear. Many specialists book months in advance, so don't wait for things to get worse before calling to schedule a test date or begin therapy, because there may be a long wait for an appointment. If you are in a hurry and the wait is long, make the appointment, but ask to be placed on a cancellation list for a possible earlier appointment.

- Before you hire a professional, try to get recommendations from other parents who have used this person. Be sure to ask about the professional's credentials or check them out online. A lot of information is easily available on the Internet, including license information from your state licensing bureau. Make sure your professional has the proper credentials. If you are working with an advocate or attorney, be sure to get their input regarding the professional you are considering.

- As you approach outside professionals, consider that you are building a team of experts to help you navigate the special education system, evaluate your child, and provide therapy. Be sure to communicate clearly with these people about your expectations and evaluate their expectations of what they can do for you. As you work with them, constantly reevaluate how they are doing. Don't hesitate to ask for more effort or switch professionals if you aren't getting what you need.

- Avoid conflicts of interest. Try to find an independent expert who has no personal, professional, or financial ties with your school district. Ask if he or she would be willing to testify on your child's behalf at a due process hearing, if necessary. Though it will likely never come to that, you may someday have to depend on their integrity and independence. See Chapter 5, "Conflicts of Interest," for more information.

- If your resources are limited and you can only hire one person, consider hiring an advocate who can help you understand the special education process, your child's evaluations and IEPs, and your rights under the law. An advocate can help you be the manager of your child's documents, can help you understand the overall "picture" of how your child is progressing in special education, and can help you plan for the future. An advocate's fee can be extremely reasonable when compared to other professionals' rates. There is also a federally financed program, Protection and Advocacy for People With Disabilities, that can provide free advocacy help. The website: www.parentcenternetwork.org contains links that will help you locate a group in your area.

CHAPTER **4**

UNDERSTANDING SCHOOL EVALUATIONS

During our years in special education we read many school evaluations: some were informative and helpful, but too many others were inadequate and sometimes even disingenuous. Why this should be is puzzling, as IDEA is very specific about the requirements for school evaluations. Perhaps it is because, while the law sets high standards for how evaluations are performed, it doesn't say much about how the resulting reports should be written. This is an area where misunderstanding and the possibility of conflict between parents and schools creep in.

The purposes of evaluations, aside from determining eligibility, are to inform parents, teachers, and other specialists about how a student's learning problems may be affecting behavior at home and/or school, the extent to which these difficulties can be remediated, and what supports or specialized instruction are needed to maximize progress and minimize the long-term impact of these difficulties.[30] Unless the evaluation is specific in its purpose, clearly describes the meaning of the testing data, and includes recommendations that are practical and comprehensive, the report will be unhelpful and possibly even damaging if it misleads parents and teachers as to the true nature of the problems a student faces.

THE REALITY OF SCHOOL EVALUATIONS

If there is one fact that parents need to be aware of regarding school evaluations, it is that the people who create them work for the school district and not for the parents. Many of these people are well meaning and want to do what is right for the student. Their hands can be tied, however, by rules and the bureaucratic process, and more subtly, by a school culture that emphasizes minimizing services to save the budget while pretending not to. School districts have been known to fire or demote school personnel who advocate too strongly for students with disabilities.[31]

We experienced the reality of school evaluations when our son was struggling in first grade. An educational evaluation showed scores in the 99th percentile for knowledge and memory and the 1st percentile for reading ability, a discrepancy that indicates a significant learning disability. From this, the school evaluator concluded that our son was "a student with a specific language disability in reading and written language." Yet in the same report the evaluator wrote that our son's problems in reading and written language were "related to his fine motor needs." While he did have difficulty with fine motor skills, the testing data clearly indicated that the primary source of his academic problems was a language-based learning disability.

When we received our son's IEP for the second grade, the language-based learning disability wasn't even mentioned. His writing problems were attributed only to a lack of fine motor skills, so the IEP focused on providing occupational therapy. The learning disability was largely ignored and our son grew more and more frustrated as he failed to keep up with his peers in the classroom. Years later an independent evaluation discovered he was several years below his grade level in written language, an unmistakable indication that he had needed more specialized (and costly) instruction for his learning disability in order to catch up and not just therapy for his fine motor deficits.

When parents are exhausted and grasping for answers, they can read reports with complicated charts, vague statements, and confusing statistics and still not fully understand their child's needs. Even if the test results in a report might not sound positive, when the evaluation concludes with statements like the ones we have seen: "It has been a pleasure working with this enthusiastic and engaging youngster," and "She is a polite and hard-working adolescent," the positive sounding ending is what parents tend to remember, rather than the reality of the data. We came to think of this phenomenon as "blind trust," an uncritical belief that the school will always speak the truth and do what is best for the child. From this and other experiences we learned that parents must not give in to blind trust. Instead, they must make the effort to understand what types of information should appear in an evaluation and how to interpret evaluations that, while technically accurate, may not be as candid about a student's actual disabilities as they should be.

WHAT TO EXPECT IN AN EVALUATION

While every evaluation should be individualized to the unique needs of the student and the specific goals of the test, there are certain types of information that should appear in any report you receive. Since IDEA contains very few requirements for the content of a written evaluation, it is likely that you will not see as much information as you might need. We have examined many school evaluations and find it frustrating when important information, conclusions, and even recommendations are inadequately addressed or even omitted. These problems don't just affect parents. They also affect classroom teachers and IEP Teams who rely on evaluations to tell them how to provide effective instruction, accommodations, and write appropriate goals for a student.

The following sections describe the information that should be in a properly written evaluation. For clarity, we have categorized this information under logical headings, but this may not be the way any reports you receive will be organized. You should, however, look for this information to be present in some form. Beyond these categories, you may also find other types of information in a report unique to the particular type of testing being performed. For example, an educational evaluation might contain a section in which the student relates his or her opinion about school and self-image that would not be part of a physical therapy evaluation.

Personal data

An evaluation should begin by providing information about the student beyond just a name, date of birth, and gender. Why has the student been referred for the evaluation? Are there observed personality traits that make the particular evaluation relevant? Usually this information is supplied through questionnaires filled out by parents and classroom teachers, and can provide important clues about the student to the examiner before the formal testing begins. Be sure that you recognize the student being described in this section and agree with the reasons for the referral. Once we had an evaluation performed by a psychologist working from teacher and parent questionnaires who misinterpreted the answers and created a profile for our son that bore no resemblance to him. The resulting evaluation was invalid and time was wasted while it was done over. Although this is a rare event in our experience, an accurate description of the student is an important part of any evaluation.

Behavioral observations

An important category of information in an evaluation is the examiner's observations of the student both before and during the test. Factors such as appearance and behavior can reflect how engaged a student is and indicate how accurate the results are. During the test, is the student confident and willing to take risks in answering questions, or uninvolved and restless, anxious and hesitant? Even factors such as grooming, dress, and eye contact with the examiner are important clues to factor into a report's conclusions. If the examiner's observations are that the student is making a sincere effort on the test, that increases the likelihood that the test results are a valid measure of the abilities being assessed.

Evaluation goals

An evaluation is performed to answer one or more questions about the student being tested. For an initial eligibility evaluation, one question might be: "Are there cognitive and/or academic weaknesses that would indicate a specific learning disability?" Relevant questions for an educational evaluation might be: "To what degree do the student's learning problems affect his/her ability to function in school?" and "What are the student's cognitive and academic developmental levels?" Other types of evaluations should have similar goals specific to the tests being administered.

Whatever the goals, the examiner should state up front the purpose and reasons for the evaluation as they apply specifically to the student being tested. While this might seem obvious, many reports we have read fail to state their goals in a clear manner, and some don't state a goal at all. This is unfortunate, since without clearly stated goals, how can parents, or even the examiner, know if the evaluation has achieved its purpose?

Test description

An evaluation should contain a description of the test or tests being administered. This is typically a standardized, boilerplate description. It is important that you understand the nature and purpose of the test. If the boilerplate is too technical or full of jargon, ask the examiner to add a clearer description you are comfortable with. Remember that you may need to refer to this report in the future and you don't want to have to puzzle over the meaning and purpose of the test.

Review of existing evaluation data

IDEA requires that the Team and qualified examiners review any previous relevant evaluations, including those performed by independent evaluators and supplied by the parents.[32] A report should acknowledge this data and indicate whether the current testing confirms or contradicts the previous data and conclusions.

Test data

Every report should include the data resulting from the testing that the examiner performed. There is not room in this chapter, nor is it our intention, to offer a tutorial on the wide variety of test scores you may encounter in your child's evaluations. You should, however, either familiarize yourself with the basics of interpreting test scores or rely on someone outside your school system, such as an experienced advocate, to help you with that interpretation. Authorities such as Pamela Darr Wright and Pete Wright consider an understanding of the Bell Curve essential to comparing scores, measuring progress, and measuring the effectiveness of various therapies and teaching techniques. Their book, *From Emotions to Advocacy*, listed in Appendix C, contains two chapters on tests and measurements and is a good place to start the process of learning what you need to know about the test data in your child's evaluations.

Later in this chapter are examples of some of the recurring problems we have seen in evaluations. These examples contain references to certain test scores. The following descriptions of these scores are not comprehensive and are meant only to help you better understand the examples.*

RAW SCORES

Raw scores indicate the actual performance on the test, whether the number of questions answered correctly on a test of academic or general knowledge, or the number of jumping jacks or other activities

---

*   In addition, Appendix A contains a table comparing these scores to the standard psychometric descriptions that are used in psychological and educational evaluations.

on a test of physical ability. Raw scores must be interpreted in one or more ways to get a valid comparison to how other students performed on the same test. For this reason it is not usually helpful to include raw scores in a report. If there is an unusual range, or "scatter" of interpreted scores, then it might make sense for parents to have a qualified outside professional examine the raw scores. Otherwise, there is no reason to expect an evaluation to include this data.

STANDARD SCORES

Standard scores are the most common method for interpreting raw scores. In this method, the average is 100 with a deviation of 15, indicating the range of possible average scores. In other words, an average standard score can range from 85 to 115.* Any score that falls lower than 85 or higher than 115 is considered atypical and is an indication that further investigation might be needed to discover why the score is outside the average range and what the implications of that score might be.

SCALED SCORES

Scaled scores group similar items into groups or subtests, such as measurements of math calculation or reading comprehension. Certain common assessments, like the Wechsler Intelligence Scale for Children (WISC), interpret the raw data as scaled scores that range from 1 to 19. An average scaled score is 10 with a standard deviation of 3. Because scaled scores are grouped by skill area, a difference between the highest and lowest scores in a subtest that fall outside the standard deviation (lower than 7 or higher than 13) can indicate a potential disability.

PERCENTILE RANK

Percentile rank is another common method for interpreting raw scores, often presented along with standard or scaled scores. In school evaluations, percentiles are used to determine the relative standing (or rank) of a student being tested in comparison to all students taking that test. For example, a percentile rank of 50 is average, meaning that 50 percent of all students taking the test scored higher and 50 percent scored lower than average. Percentile ranks between 25 and 75 are considered to be in the average range. Note that percentile ranks are

---

* Some professionals feel that a more useful range of average standard scores is 90 to 109.

not the same as the percentage of a student's right or wrong answers on the test.

GRADE AND AGE EQUIVALENT SCORES

Grade equivalent scores indicate the grade level of students who, on average, get a particular raw score. For example, if a fifth grade student achieves a raw score on a math test that is the same as that of an average fourth grade student, then the grade equivalent for that student in math is the fourth grade. Usually the grade equivalent number is further refined by adding the month that the student is in that grade, such as 3.9 for a third grader in the ninth, or last month of third grade.

Educators and some psychologists tend not to like grade equivalent scores, complaining that while they present an overall approximation of achievement, they don't fully show a student's strengths and weaknesses, nor do they necessarily indicate that a student is doing work at that grade level.* While there is some justification for this point of view, parents are likely to find grade equivalent scores the most easily understood way to recognize a potential learning disability. Any grade level score that is more than one year below a child's current grade in school is an indication of a developmental delay that needs further investigation.

Similar to grade level scores, age equivalent scores compare a student's performance to age groups whose average scores are in the same range. If a student is significantly younger or older than his or her grade level peers, then age equivalent scores can help explain a below or above average grade level score. For example, in a test of physical fitness, if a student scores below grade level it would be relevant to consider that student's age equivalent score. A younger student with a low grade level score in a test of physical ability might have an average, or even an above average, age equivalent score based on the same raw score.

STATISTICALLY SIGNIFICANT DISCREPANCIES

The diagnosis of most learning disabilities occurs when there is a large difference between a specific ability, like reading, writing, or math calculation, and a student's general ability as measured by an IQ test or age and grade level expectations. There are somewhat complex

---

* One teachers' college even goes so far as to advise its teachers-in-training that when talking with parents they should "never use grade equivalent scores in a way that hints that they have any validity."[33]

mathematical formulas used to calculate which differences fall within a normal range and which are large enough to indicate a disability. However, when a student's IQ falls in the average or above average range and performance on an ability test is below the average range, it is generally reasonable to consider that a statistically significant discrepancy.

Conclusions

Sometimes labeled "Summary" or "Impressions," the conclusions in an evaluation should be based on the testing data and, at a minimum, answer the questions posed in the evaluation goals. The conclusions should also address all the meaningful testing data, not just a limited subset. We have seen evaluations in which significant discrepancies that appear in the data are never mentioned in the conclusions. For more on this issue, see the section "Ignoring, hiding, or minimizing a statistically significant discrepancy" later in this chapter.

You should expect the conclusions to clearly describe both strengths and weaknesses. We have seen many evaluations stress a student's strengths and minimize the weaknesses, something that most parents want to hear, but that does not help them understand their child's disability or help them get appropriate services. Likewise, if any conclusions are written in unclear technical terms or jargon, ask that they be translated into understandable English.

Recommendations

No evaluation is complete without clear, detailed recommendations for the school to implement based on the report's conclusions. Many states, including ours, require that school evaluations contain specific recommendations on how to meet the needs of the student (be sure to check the laws in your state). These recommendations are essential to create an effective program for special education teachers and specialists to follow and should form the basis of a student's IEP goals (see Chapter 7, "Writing Effective IEP Goals").

Once, when our son was in elementary school, we got a speech and language evaluation with this single recommendation: "He may need modifications within a large group/classroom setting to address his attentional needs." The examiner, a speech and language pathologist working for the school, didn't name even one specific modification or accommodation for the classroom teacher to follow.

Examiner's signature and credentials

If an examiner feels that the testing and conclusions are valid, it is reasonable to expect him or her to certify the validity of the evaluation by signing the written report. Although we have seen only one evaluation out of dozens that did not contain the name of the examiner, we have seen many in which the person conducting the test did not sign the document. A signature is an important indication that the person giving the test is willing to stand behind its methodology and conclusions.

About a third of the evaluations we have read do not list the examiner's credentials, or just identify the examiner as a "teacher." IDEA expects all evaluators to be qualified, and there is no reason why their credentials should not be documented on the report next to the examiner's name. You, and everyone else who reads and relies on an evaluation, have a right to this information.

READING A SCHOOL EVALUATION

Even when an evaluation contains all the information we have described, it may still be difficult to understand. We have read many school reports that do not clearly explain the testing data and seem to expect the reader to have an advanced knowledge of statistical analysis. Other reports are full of technical terms that might have meaning to professionals but are unfamiliar to most parents. Even worse are evaluations containing jargon that is virtually meaningless, such as one report that observed: "...the Performance I.Q. does not represent a unitary concept" and "[student's]* Verbal I.Q. is not a unitary construct." No effort was made in this report to explain the meaning of a "unitary concept" or a "unitary construct." We have also seen evaluations that accurately describe significant discrepancies between strong ability and weak achievement, but on the same page say that there is no academic or learning problem. In still others, there is nothing in writing documenting a diagnosis or there are inconclusive

---

*　We have removed all student names from the quoted passages and corrected the grammar where necessary.

statements, vague phrases, and very little useful information. Some school psychologists claim that they cannot diagnose learning disabilities in an evaluation,[34] but there is no legal reason why this should be so. Ethically, in fact, they are obligated to provide a "clear diagnosis with supporting evidence."[35]

The following sections describe some of the misleading statements and conclusions we have found in school evaluations. We have seen these kinds of statements over and over in both our son's evaluations and those that other parents have received. You are likely to see similar statements in your child's evaluations and should be prepared to ask questions when you do.

Ignoring, hiding, or minimizing a statistically significant discrepancy

Something we have seen over and over is that significant discrepancies are reported in an evaluation without stating that the discrepancy might indicate a learning disability. A classic example in one school evaluation read: "A statistically significant discrepancy is observed between [student's] Verbal and Performance Indices, with the Performance Index falling thirty-five points below the Verbal Index." The report makes no further mention of this discrepancy or what it might mean. Contrast this with a similar evaluation performed by an outside evaluator chosen by the parents: "There remains a statistically significant difference (36 points) between [verbal cognitive ability and visual-spatial ability], consistent with [student's] diagnosis of NLD [Non-Verbal Learning Disorder]." The outside evaluation clearly states the significance of the discrepancy while the school evaluation essentially ignores it.

Other evaluations "hide" discrepancies in large quantities of data. One high school student had an 83-point percentile difference between math calculation and math fluency as shown in a full page table of scores, but the examiner's conclusions commented only on the higher of the two scores, writing: "[student's] performance is high average in mathematics..." and "No discrepancies were found among [student's] achievement areas." There was only one recommendation at the end of this report and that was for an accommodation that the student be given extra time when taking tests. Nowhere in this report did the examiner write about a math disability or what specialized instruction that student might need for it.

Examples of minimizing discrepancies included one elementary school report that measured a 60-point percentile difference between verbal and perceptual skills, but called it an "imbalance in functioning," a vague phrase that doesn't appear in the diagnostic criteria of the American Psychiatric Association[36] and is not recognized as a qualifying disability in IDEA. In another evaluation, the student scored in the 21st percentile on a test of listening comprehension, which is normally considered "low average." The school examiner, however, claimed it was in the average range by adding a note next to this score that defined the average range for percentile ranks as between 16 and 84 instead of the more accepted 25 to 75.

About half of the many evaluations we have seen, mostly written by school psychologists, mention that one or more statistically significant discrepancies exist without explicitly saying that it might be connected to a learning disability. While not a technical violation of IDEA, such practices are frowned upon by other members of the profession. One expert in child psychology puts it clearly: "In their reports, psychologists should make their hypotheses about the child's difficulties explicit."[37]

Testing data that doesn't appear in the IEP

Some school evaluations contain testing results that aren't mentioned in the student's IEP. One evaluation we encountered showed a student testing with a wide scattering of scores, several below grade level in important subject areas and several above grade level. In describing the testing data, the student's IEP omitted the low scores and referred only to the high scores, concluding that the student had "outstanding academic skills."

A student's IEP should reflect the results of all pertinent testing data and include measurable goals addressing all problem areas identified by the testing. For more information about how IEP goals should be written, see Chapter 7, "Writing Effective IEP Goals."

Blame the student or the family

We have seen many school evaluations conclude by saying that a student's learning problems are a result of low self-esteem, social isolation, lack of sleep, family stress, depression, anxiety, or other personal problems. One evaluator wrote that a student's self-image contributed to his poor test results rather than acknowledge a learning disability that had been identified for this student in testing years earlier.

In six educational evaluations of different students, written over a three-year span by the same examiner, there was a section at the beginning titled "Self-Report" in which the student was asked to describe him or herself. In a striking coincidence, the second paragraph of each self-report begins with a sentence describing a positive quality about the student, like "attentive to details," "highly organized," "always finishes the work she starts," and "always remembers what he is supposed to do." Then, in all six evaluations, the next sentence reads: "In contrast, some reported behaviors may be inhibiting [student's] cognitive performance," followed by an identical list of problems: "careless mistakes," "difficulty concentrating," and "easily distracted." Two of the reports also added an additional problem: "forgets what she is supposed to do" or "loses his personal belongings." Is the examiner implying that the learning problems revealed later in the testing data are the result of these "inhibiting" behaviors rather than a learning disability? None of the conclusions in these reports mention a specific learning disability. Does the boilerplate list of problems really apply to each individual student or does it reveal a bias on the part of the examiner about the source of the student's problems?

This is not an isolated incident. A 1988 study of 5,000 student evaluations written by school psychologists found that virtually all 5,000 reports concluded that either the student, the family, or both, were the cause of the student's learning problems. With some apparent irony, the study observed: "If only these districts had better functioning children with a few more supportive parents, there would be no educational difficulties."[38] There is more about the implications of this study in Chapter 5, "Conflicts of Interest."

Words and phrases that obscure the true meaning

Language, as we know, can be used to hide meaning as well as reveal it. In our readings of school evaluations we have seen many examples of hiding meaning behind words. "Relative" appears to be the adjective of choice for this task. In one psychological evaluation of a middle schooler the phrase "relative weakness" appears ten times (five times on a single page) along with a single use of "relative deficiencies" to describe different skill areas. For grammatical variety the adverb form appears as well, with the phrases "relatively lower scores" and "relatively better" appearing once each. Although the term "relative weakness" can be a valid way to describe a skill that, while not low in an absolute sense, is low compared to other measured abilities, this report never bothers to explain what the weaknesses, deficiencies, or lower scores are relative to.*

Another phrase we have seen used to describe below grade level performance in an evaluation is "processing impairment." Processing impairment is not recognized as a qualifying disability by IDEA except when caused by a traumatic brain injury "acquired...by an external physical force,"[39] which did not apply to the student being examined. In this evaluation, the student reported that many of the skills tested were "very difficult" or "impossible" to perform and the test results showed a wide scatter of high and low test scores, a clear indication of a potential learning disability. Yet, the examiner concluded the report by writing that the student's academic skills were "within normal limits" and "average." Combining terminology that lacks a clear legal definition with conclusions that include phrases like "normal limits" and "average" can mislead the unwary reader. If the parents of this student only focused on the vague terminology and the conclusion, they might not understand that the testing revealed indications of genuine disabilities and might even think that their child had no significant learning problems.

Cut and paste results

In reading one group of evaluations we were puzzled when we came across descriptions of five different students, all written by the same examiner, containing these identical and seemingly contradictory sentences: "[Student's] math calculation skill is advanced. [He/She] gave incorrect responses on math calculation items involving fractions, percentages, algebra, geometry, and advanced mathematics." These were students in three different grades in high school. We then came across a sixth evaluation containing the exact same sentences except that the student had scored in the low average range in math calculation. The sentences: "[Student's] math calculation skill is in the low average range. [He/She] gave incorrect responses on math

---

* While many professions use technical terms that have a meaning specific to that field, such "terms of art" are often confusing to those outside that profession. When writing for the lay public it is the responsibility of the professional to either avoid such jargon or explain it for the uninitiated.

calculation items involving fractions, percentages, algebra, geometry, and advanced mathematics," finally made sense.

It became clear that the examiner had simply copied the sentences from one evaluation to another without even proofreading them for accuracy. More disturbing was the realization that the parents who received the first five evaluations had accepted these statements without apparently questioning them and having the report corrected.

No written recommendations or inadequate recommendations

We have read many evaluations that end with a summary but no recommendations on how the school can help the student. Sometimes only minimal recommendations are made, such as "additional time on tests," "counseling," or "repeat directions." For students with complex needs, these sorts of recommendations do not contain enough information for the school staff or parents to effectively help the student. Such reports ignore the requirement that evaluations provide "strategies that provide relevant information that directly assists persons in determining the educational needs of the child."[40]

Another common practice is to conclude a report with: "Specific recommendations will be discussed at the Team meeting." In these reports, the evaluator is passing the responsibility of making recommendations on to the people who will attend the upcoming meeting. While the Team may discuss recommendations, it is easy to forget or ignore the details of a discussion. Without something in writing, it is almost guaranteed that any verbal recommendations will not be acted upon. For more about what you should expect in writing and how to obtain it, see Chapter 9, "The Paper Trail."

Changing the subject

When all else fails, an evaluation can apply a little misdirection to divert the focus from a student's weaknesses. When our son was struggling to read in elementary school and was falling behind in all the subject areas that required reading, we received an evaluation that began with the sentence that he had "…made wonderful progress academically, behaviorally, and emotionally over the last year." Of course, this was what stuck in our minds, and as a result the low scores in significant skill areas seemed to concern us a little less.

Combined with a healthy dose of compliments like calling him "hard-working," and a "hard worker," we were less inclined to ask the difficult questions about how far behind our son was academically and what he needed to catch up. We only realized later that these phrases are often simply euphemisms to describe a student who, in reality, is struggling in school. It can't be lost on the school evaluators that these phrases will be more easily misinterpreted by parents as positive attributes than a direct statement that a student's skills are significantly below grade level.

THE ALTERNATIVE: INDEPENDENT EDUCATIONAL EVALUATIONS

As described in Chapter 3, "Outside Professionals," you have the option of hiring your own expert to perform evaluations. In situations where there is reason to doubt the completeness or objectivity of a school evaluation, an independent professional can perform an evaluation free of any perceived bias that might be the source of your doubt. IDEA refers to these types of evaluations as Independent Educational Evaluations, or IEE. Despite the name, an IEE is not limited to an evaluation of academic skills.* An IEE should, of course, contain at least as much detail and information as we recommend for school evaluations. While most of the IEE reports we have examined do, we have also seen incomplete and questionable IEEs. If you carefully research an outside professional and explain to that person beforehand what kind of information you are expecting in a report, this should not be a problem.

Private evaluations can be expensive. Parents can request that their school district pay for an IEE if they disagree with the results of a school evaluation or if the school will not perform an evaluation in "all areas of suspected disability."[42] The school must then either file a due process complaint notice to show that their evaluation (or refusal to perform an evaluation) was appropriate, or pay for the IEE.[43] While this sounds good in theory, in practice it can be the cause of delays or even an expensive due process hearing. To complicate matters, some states place limits on how much they will pay for a publicly funded IEE. If time is important, and in special education it usually is, you will probably have to pay for an IEE yourself. An alternative

---

* Federal regulations define an IEE only as "an evaluation conducted by a qualified examiner who is not employed by the public agency responsible for the education of the child in question."[41]

is to get low-cost outside evaluations through colleges and university psychology or education departments. It may take some effort to locate an appropriate institution, but it is worth doing.

WHAT PARENTS CAN DO

Here is a list of suggestions on how you can use the information in this chapter:

- Provide the school with a written list of all the disabilities you suspect and want to have assessed. See Chapter 9, "The Paper Trail," for the reasons why you should make all your requests in writing. The school is required to perform the appropriate assessments and the resulting evaluations should clearly state whether or not there is a diagnosis of a disability in each of these areas.

- Learn how to interpret test scores so that you have an accurate picture of your child without the filter of the evaluator's conclusions influencing you. Learn about the different methods of interpreting testing data, bell curves, and standard deviations, and how they indicate the presence of learning disabilities. The resources listed in Appendix C provide a good place to start. If you do not feel comfortable interpreting test data, then consider hiring an experienced advocate to read the evaluations and help you understand what they mean.

- Make sure that the report identifies the specific disability if the testing data indicates that one exists. Question vague labels like "relative weakness," "imbalance in functioning," or "processing impairment." Terms like these aren't defined in special education law as a disability and can make it harder to get appropriate services for your child. If the school's evaluation does not clearly diagnose a disability (or the lack of one), then you should request additional testing.

- Make sure that evaluations conclude with specific, detailed recommendations for helping your child learn and progress to grade level if appropriate. The recommendations should be prioritized in importance and provide meaningful direction for teachers and other school personnel who work with your child. The recommendations should include needed services or even the type of placement, not just classroom accommodations. If you get an evaluation that has inadequate or no recommendations, or says "Specific recommendations will be discussed at the Team meeting," ask that recommendations be added to the report before your Team meets to discuss it.

- The most important clues as to whether or not an evaluation is giving you an accurate picture of your child are found by comparing the testing data to the evaluation's conclusions and recommendations. When they don't appear to match up, you need to ask questions, dig deeper, and above all, not give in to blind trust. With luck, you may need just a little more explanation from the evaluator. We have found that anything that is even a little ambiguous or vague in a report can be misunderstood by parents and teachers.

- Question language that appears to obscure or "sugarcoat" your child's difficulties. While it may be well intentioned on the part of school evaluators, not dealing directly with a child's disability only serves to make the process of obtaining appropriate services more difficult and delays getting help for your child.

- Make sure that all important testing data and recommendations from evaluations (including IEEs) are included in your child's IEP. This is the document from which goals, services, accommodations, and modifications are developed and it is your legal contract with the school. If the results and recommendations of an evaluation are not written into the IEP, then they won't help your child. See Chapter 6, "The IEP: Powerful Tool or Worthless Paper?" for where this information should go.

- Do not accept a report that is not signed by the examiner or does not indicate that the examiner is qualified to perform the evaluation.

- Consider having an independent educational evaluation (IEE) performed if you disagree with the school district's evaluation of your child. Parents can have an IEE done at private expense at any time. Know your rights under IDEA and your state regulations regarding an IEE done at public expense.

CHAPTER 5

CONFLICTS OF INTEREST

One troubling aspect of special education is the possibility of a conflict between the needs of your child and the interests of the people working with your child. While you may think that a school employee considers the needs of your child first, you must always be aware that when there is a conflict between what is appropriate for your child and the needs of the school district, it is very possible that your child's needs will be considered second. Conflicts of interest can even occur with the outside professionals you hire or are considering hiring. This sort of conflict is less understandable than with school employees and has even less justification given the codes of ethics that certain professional societies require of their members.

Ultimately, there is no sure way to prevent a conflict of interest from occurring. Most of these situations are usually hidden for the simple reason that they are unethical at best and illegal at worst. Unless you learn to ask the right questions and approach situations with open eyes, you may never even realize that you have encountered a conflict of interest.

CONFLICTS FOR SCHOOL EMPLOYEES

As we gradually discovered during our years in special education, many of the educators working with our son had to decide between what was best for him and what was best for their jobs. This is primarily a result of how special education services are funded. The very people who recommend and approve services are frequently the same people who control the school district budget or who are working for those who control the budget. If a potential service is too involved and costly, a school employee is less likely to recommend it, regardless of how beneficial it might be for the student.

According to IDEA, special education is need-based, which means that if a student needs a service in order to get an appropriate education, the student is supposed to receive it. There must be no cost to the parents, and the school district should not consider cost in its decision. Sadly, this ideal is frequently in conflict with reality.

Always bear in mind that the real client of a school employee working with your son or daughter is the school district, not you or your child. Many professionals employed by the district will not act in the best interest of the child if the financial or personal cost is too high. For those school employees who might be tempted to act otherwise, there are many examples of what this might cost them. In 2009, a school psychologist in Massachusetts filed a complaint against his school district with the Office of Civil Rights because a student had not received a social/emotional evaluation even though that student had twice attempted suicide. After the psychologist filed his complaint, the school department and the town's school committee placed him on an involuntary leave of absence and required that he be examined by a psychiatrist as a condition for returning to work.[44]

CONFLICTS FOR OUTSIDE PROFESSIONALS

Whenever you consider hiring a professional, take a careful look at the potential conflicts of interest that this person might have with your school district. The fact that you are paying for the professional's time yourself does not always guarantee objective or even appropriate advice or services. Perhaps the prospect of future referrals from the school district or even possible future employment in that district might cloud a professional's judgement.

There might be an even less obvious relationship with the school district that prevents a professional from accurately presenting your child's case for needed services. The conflict may be subtle and largely innocent, as when a professional has children in the same school as your child. The professional may have developed a relationship with certain teachers or administrators in the course of his or her child's education and may be unfairly biased toward believing that these people are providing your child appropriate services, even when that is not the case. Or, the professional may not advocate as strongly as he or she might otherwise for fear that such efforts may have consequences for his or her own children.

We discovered the possibility of just such a conflict of interest in an evaluation written by an independent educational psychologist that also appears to have violated a state law. This professional had previously worked in our town's school system and had a child who attended the public schools. While our state special education law prohibits evaluators from recommending placement in "specific classrooms or schools,"[45] this professional's first recommendation began: "[Student]* may be best placed at the high school..." The other recommendations then used several phrases in describing the suggested placement that closely echoed the school district's descriptions of programs that it offers students in special education. Was it a coincidence that the recommendation from this former school employee was for a program that the district already had in place and would cost less than an alternative placement outside the school district? It is impossible to know with certainty, just as it is impossible to know whether this professional was aware of the law that prohibited her from recommending a specific school placement, but avoiding a conflict of interest involves avoiding the appearance of a conflict as much as it does avoiding an actual conflict. Nevertheless, this professional's recommendations put this student's parents in a potentially awkward position. If they believed that their child would be better placed in a setting other than the public high school, the recommendations would have made their case for outside placement much more difficult.

AN ETHICAL DILEMMA

An article written in 1988 by Galen Alessi, a psychologist and professor at Western Michigan University, "Diagnosis Diagnosed: A Systemic Reaction," illustrates the ethical dilemma facing school psychologists.[46] Alessi writes about a survey he took of 50 school psychologists from around the country, each of whom had handled approximately 100 cases during the previous school year. That yielded 5,000 case studies. The goal was to determine the cause of learning and behavior problems in children.

The survey identified five possible causes of problems: faulty curriculum or the child being misplaced in the curriculum, ineffective teaching practices, ineffective management practices by the school administration, lack of parental support, and a student's physical or psychological problems. All the school psychologists agreed that each of the five factors could play a role in a student not learning properly or having behavior problems in school.

---

*   As in other chapters, actual names have been replaced with [student].

When the evaluations were examined, all 5,000 concluded that the student's physical or psychological problems were the primary cause of the learning and behavior problems. Between 500 to 1000 (10% to 20%) also concluded that home factors or lack of parental support were a contributing factor. None of the evaluations stated that the cause of the student's problems was the curriculum, teaching, or administrative practices.

When asked, most of the psychologists in the survey reported that "informal school policy (or 'school culture') dictates that conclusions be restricted to child and family factors." Many of the psychologists said that they could lose their jobs or would be made to feel professionally uncomfortable if they blamed school-related factors.

The article concludes with the questions:

> Are we really helping children by concluding that the children alone are responsible for educational problems? Are we helping the school system at the expense of the children? How do we balance the rights of those who pay for our services against the rights of those who receive our services, when interests clash?

Although these are questions meant for school psychologists, parents should carefully consider their implications when dealing with all school professionals.

OUR EXPERIENCE WITH CONFLICTING INTERESTS

We have heard from many parents who have told us convincing stories of school employees who placed personal or school interests above the best interests of their child. In one case that affected us directly, we believe an outside professional traded her silence about our son's needs in exchange for employment in our school district, benefiting personally from not recommending an outside placement.

After our son had experienced a particularly difficult year in middle school, he was seen over the summer by a psychologist at an agency in another town. This agency contracted with our school district to provide counseling services at no cost to parents when the director of special education recommended it. Although we did not initially have that arrangement, we decided to pay the agency on our own to have one of the staff, a Dr. X,* evaluate and provide counseling for our son.

---

*   Not the initial of her real name.

Dr. X's evaluation indicated that the school needed to provide services more intensive than they had been, and as the new school year was about to begin, she assured us that she would attend Team meetings and advocate for our son to see that his IEP was followed, something that hadn't happened the previous year. When the fall school term began, the school district offered to continue the sessions with Dr. X as part of our son's IEP services, so we were delighted. As the school year progressed, it became obvious that the public school was not meeting his needs. Though she attended Team Meetings, Dr. X never seemed to advocate strongly for more appropriate services for our son. In a private meeting toward the end of the school year, however, Dr. X told us that she would not hesitate to recommend an outside placement to the district's director of special education if we asked her to.

The job interview

About a year later, after we had placed our son unilaterally at a private special education school, we scheduled a meeting with our school district to discuss why this had been necessary and to seek reimbursement. We asked Dr. X to attend and speak about why she felt an outside placement was important. She agreed, contingent upon receiving payment for an hour of her time at her usual rate. At her request, we mailed a check directly to her prior to the meeting.

As the meeting began, Dr. X announced that she had to leave shortly for another meeting. She then proceeded to speak in very positive terms about our son's experience in middle school, contradicting her private comments to us and the conclusions of her evaluation. She did not recommend an outside placement. After ten minutes Dr. X left the room, unavailable to make further comments or answer questions.

Shocked by this, we wrote a letter that night to Dr. X questioning her behavior. We received a defensive reply in which she justified her actions and revealed that she had discussed our meeting with the director of special education ahead of time, though she didn't explain the nature of that conversation. Dr. X had felt no responsibility to get our permission to have this prior discussion with the director or even inform us of it, despite the fact that she had contracted with us directly. Even more troubling, it turned out that the check Dr. X had requested was never cashed, and because Dr. X had asked to have the check sent directly to her and not to the agency's business manager, there was no record that it had ever been received.

Five months later we learned that Dr. X had left the private agency to become a guidance counselor for one of the schools in our district. We finally understood that all along there had been a conflict of interest between her desire to work directly for the school district and her professional responsibility to our son. It is hard to escape the conclusion that her behavior at the last meeting had been nothing more than a job interview, since by then she must have already submitted her application for her new job. It appears that she had used this meeting to prove to the director of special education that she could be relied upon to contain the school's budget at the expense of her clients and their families.

Not an isolated instance

A short time later a mother approached us for advice about a similar situation. Her son was having great difficulty in high school and she desperately wanted him in a private special education school. She was taking him to the same agency for counseling that we had used, so we told her about our experience. At her son's next appointment, she asked the therapist if he thought her son needed an outside placement. He said yes and even mentioned which schools might be a good fit. When she asked the therapist if he would repeat his comments at a Team meeting, he refused, explaining that his salary was dependent on the school district's contract with his agency. This mother then terminated her relationship with that therapist and began to take her son to someone who was truly independent.

Had we fully understood the implications of the financial and employment relationship between the private agency and the school district, we never would have used their services.* The hard lesson is that if a professional has a financial or even a personal connection to a school district, their opinions and behavior may be influenced by that relationship.

---

*   To compound the indignity, the agency is a non-profit institution and regularly asks the parents of its clients for contributions, which we gave until we realized what was going on.

DEALING WITH CONFLICTS OF INTEREST

There is ample literature on how certain professionals, such as lawyers and psychologists, government agencies, and non-profit organizations, can avoid problems with conflicts of interest. In many cases there are laws or formal codes of ethics to guide these individuals and organizations. For example, Appendix A of the Internal Revenue Service form 1023 contains a sample conflict of interest policy for tax exempt organizations. Unfortunately, the problems that parents encounter with conflicts of interest in special education do not have such obvious solutions.

In fact, your school district and any agencies that contract with the district for special education services probably have a written code of ethics that prohibit behavior that would result in a conflict of interest. They do this by spelling out what constitutes a conflict and the ways it should be avoided, such as through disclosure or recusal. We have read department of education codes of ethics for several states and our local school district, and while each one is full of high-minded prose, none of them address what happens when a school district is faced with a budget that precludes giving the special education students in its charge an appropriate education. Instead, the codes we have read address issues such as teachers not accepting gifts from students over a certain value, or the appropriateness of teachers having their expenses paid on school trips.

The problem is that public school teachers and special education administrators serve a number of constituencies and have a variety of obligations to multiple clients that include the school superintendent, school board, and the community as a whole, and not just students and parents. When a teacher or administrator encounters a situation in which the needs of one of these constituents conflicts with the needs of a student, it is almost always the student who takes a back seat. For example, the need to control the school budget almost always takes precedence over a student's need for costly services. It is even easy for school personnel to rationalize that there is no real harm in doing this. After all, a young student who is struggling will doubtless gain maturity in the coming years, so that any current lack of progress due to not providing adequate services will ultimately correct itself. This notion is especially appealing when it will be some other teacher in the next grade who has the responsibility for helping the child. And most important, recommending services that are not authorized by one's superiors is a good way for a teacher or school specialist to find the way to the unemployment line. The slide down this slope is all too predictable and very much against both the letter and spirit of IDEA. Yet the pressure to place other needs over a student's needs is systemic in special education, both subtle and intense at the same time.

WHAT PARENTS CAN DO

Here is a list of suggestions on how you can use the information in this chapter:

- Realize that there are many well-meaning school employees who have a strong sense of ethics and dedication to children with special needs. Rarely, however, are they the ones who have the ability to authorize services or accommodations that will cost the school a significant amount of money. As a result, many school employees fear speaking the truth about students because of possible retaliation from the school.[47] Try to work cooperatively with these people, realizing their limitations, as together you might be able to come up with creative solutions that allow your child to get appropriate services without triggering budgetary alarms.

- Before you hire an outside professional, try to determine what personal, financial, or professional ties they might have to your school district. Consider asking the following questions:

  o Does the professional receive any money, directly or indirectly, from the school district?

  o Does the professional get referrals from the school district or does the professional expect to get any?

  o Does the professional have children in the school district?

  o Will the professional attend Team meetings and advocate for your child?

  o If necessary, is the professional willing to attend a mediation or a due process hearing to testify on your child's behalf and to advocate for appropriate services or placement for your child, even if it might be in opposition to the school district?

- Obtain a copy of your school district's code of ethics and study it. Most districts post their code on their website, or you can ask for a copy from the school office. At the least, it will show you what your school formally expects from its employees. Don't expect it to cover the sorts of problems described in this chapter, however. These conflicts are systemic to all school districts and are rarely, if ever, openly acknowledged.

- Likewise, obtain copies of the code of ethics for any organizations in which professionals who work with your child may be members. These are usually available from those organization's websites. Lawyers, psychologists, and psychiatrists, in particular, have very strong professional codes. If your professional is licensed by your state, that gives you an additional avenue for filing a complaint if you believe that a breach of the code has occurred. Be aware that a formal complaint is both a time-consuming and difficult process to pursue, and that your time may be better spent finding more ethical professionals to work with your child.

CHAPTER **6**

THE IEP

The Individualized Education Program, or IEP, is the cornerstone of special education. It is a complex, legally binding document intended to provide a clear picture of a student's current abilities and needs, and to outline special education services for that student. The IEP can be a powerful tool for insuring that a student gets an appropriate education. It can also be ineffective if it isn't written well or if teachers and school specialists ignore it or don't have the time to study and implement it properly. We have experienced both the power and the impotence of IEPs, and in the process we have learned some things that can help you access the power of the IEP and avoid common mistakes that make it less effective.

WHAT KEEPS AN IEP FROM BEING EFFECTIVE

An IEP is powerful when it clearly describes the steps necessary to provide an appropriate education to a student with special needs and to determine when that student is making genuine progress. An IEP becomes ineffective when it lacks specifics about a student's strengths and weaknesses, goals, and the services and accommodations the student needs to make progress toward those goals. While the IEP does not offer a guarantee of progress, it is a contract that promises your school district will make a good faith effort to help your child reach his or her goals. Unfortunately, we have found that the school culture encourages a number of practices we call "school rules" that can undermine the power of an IEP.

The school rules of IEPs

Despite the fact that IDEA requires all IEPs to contain "measurable annual goals,"[48] one of the unwritten school rules we discovered is to create goals that may sound good, but are difficult to measure. For many years our son had IEP goals such as "He will improve self-confidence" or "He will experiment with voice activated technology." They seemed appropriate at first glance, but they were vague and there was no effective way to tell when or how he might meet those goals. It took a long time before we realized that when a goal is not measurable, it is possible to say that a student has achieved that goal without the student making any actual progress. Believing that your child has achieved a goal might make you feel good, but if it isn't real progress, it doesn't help your child.

Another school rule is to make it difficult for teachers to follow an IEP by limiting or even denying teachers' access to it. Some schools give classroom teachers just the IEP pages outlining accommodations and modifications. Other schools incorrectly claim that confidentiality laws prohibit them from sharing any parts of an IEP with teachers.[49] A properly written IEP contains important and specialized information that teachers and special education staff need to work effectively with a student, and the IEP should be fully available to them.

When our son was in middle school, his math teacher would give him several weeks of assignments at once rather than breaking the assignments down into smaller units as specified in his IEP. As a result, he felt overwhelmed and didn't know how to proceed. It was clear that the teacher was not implementing the accommodations in his IEP. After we emailed the teacher to ask if she had studied our son's IEP and would give smaller, more frequent math assignments, our son's liaison called us. He was angry at us for asking that the math teacher read and follow the IEP and complained that we were being "accusatory." He gave no explanation why our son's IEP accommodations had been ignored.

The IEP vs. a 504 Plan

A third school rule deserves a more detailed explanation. It is to offer a student a 504 Plan* instead of an IEP. A 504 Plan is named after Section 504 of The Rehabilitation Act of 1973, a law preventing discrimination against people with disabilities. It guarantees that students with disabilities have access to school buildings and school activities. This means that a student in a wheelchair, for example, must

---

*   Some schools call a 504 Plan an "Individualized Accommodation Plan" or IAP.

be able to enter the school building with appropriate ramps and doors and must be included in all school functions, like field trips, that are available to a student without a disability.

There are significant differences between an IEP and a 504 Plan, however. Unlike IDEA, Section 504 does not require a written plan similar to an IEP, and it guarantees a student only an education comparable to the education that students without disabilities receive. This means that a student may have fewer rights and protections under Section 504 than under IDEA, which provides an incentive for schools to place students on a 504 Plan rather than an IEP.

RIGHTS THAT ARE LACKING IN A 504 PLAN

Under IDEA, schools have certain legal obligations to students who are on IEPs that a 504 Plan lacks. On an IEP, schools must provide specialized instruction and appropriate services to prepare students for further education, employment, and independent living. This education must meet the student's unique needs and provide educational benefit. While the Section 504 statute does require schools to provide students an appropriate education, it does not define a student's rights as strictly as IDEA. This gives schools more latitude in what services they can offer or protections they have to provide.

For example, if parents go to a due process hearing at their state department of education, under IDEA an impartial person will select a hearing officer for their case. Under Section 504, in most states the school district can appoint the hearing officer. Given that the school district has a stake in how a case is decided, this may constitute a conflict of interest. Other rights under IDEA that are lacking under Section 504 include the right to participate in all Team meetings and the right to obtain an independent educational evaluation (IEE) at the school's expense.

Another difference is that under Section 504, major decisions about a student, such as evaluations and placement options, do not require the written consent of parents. Schools can even make these decisions without holding a meeting with the parents; they only have to notify parents that they have made a decision. By contrast, when a student is on an IEP, schools must include parents as full participants in any meetings where decisions affecting a student's education are made. Some states and school districts do have formal policies providing additional safeguards for students on 504 plans similar to IDEA, but these are not required and they are not universal.

DEVELOPING AN IEP

Once a student is determined to be eligible for special education as described in Chapter 1, "Getting Started in Special Education," a Team, composed of the parents, at least one representative of the school district, and a teacher,* writes an IEP to meet the student's unique needs. The IEP should clearly describe the specialized instruction, related services, modifications, and accommodations that the student will receive, and how that student's progress will be evaluated. By law, parents are equal participants in a Team meeting and they should work with the Team to write the IEP and approve it. (See Chapter 8, "Team Meetings," for more details about a parent's role.) If a student will turn 16 during the time that the IEP is in effect, the student must also be invited to participate.

IDEA requires that the IEP be reviewed and updated each school year† to reflect the student's current strengths and weaknesses, and to develop measurable goals for the coming year. These goals can only be changed with the parents' input and approval. Every three years the school must reevaluate the student to determine how much progress has been made and if he or she is still eligible for special education services. A reevaluation can occur more frequently if parents or teachers feel one is needed and request it.

School obligations once the IEP is written

Once the IEP is complete and all parties have approved it, the school district has an obligation to make sure that all of a student's teachers and service providers have access to copies and are fully informed about any accommodations or modifications they are responsible for implementing. That is why IDEA requires the IEP to be completed and put into effect at the beginning of each school year.[51] Each state has its own timeline for how quickly the IEP should be ready for parental review after a meeting. For example, our state requires a completed IEP to be ready for parental approval within two weeks, or if parents request it, within three to five calendar days of the IEP meeting.[52] Other states might require a different number of days or define their

---

* These are the minimum number of participants required by IDEA.[50] Usually a Team is composed of additional specialists and teachers.

† IDEA-04 authorized an experimental "three year" IEP that some states have instituted as a pilot program. Given how rapidly a young child develops and needs change, it is hard to understand how such a long-term IEP could be useful.

timeline in working days or school days instead of calendar days. Regardless of how the timeline is defined, the school district must keep to this schedule so teachers and service providers for the next school year have time to study the IEP and understand their roles in implementing it.

Our school district routinely delayed completing IEPs while the director of special education personally read and authorized every word of every IEP in the district, almost 500 in all. This resulted in IEPs being weeks to months late. Our son's eighth grade IEP was delayed for over five months and wasn't ready until January of that school year. This caused a delay in his receiving services that the Team had approved in the winter of the previous school year. Without a current IEP, his teachers followed the services from his outdated seventh grade IEP. Since we didn't know that there was a specific deadline for completing the IEP, we patiently and needlessly waited.

WHAT IDEA REQUIRES

Since the IEP is supposed to be individualized, there is no standard format or structure for the document.* Even though the law leaves the final format up to individual states, IDEA requires that every IEP contain the following information:

- The student's present levels of achievement and functional performance that describe how a student's disability affects his or her ability to access the school program.

- The student's annual measurable goals.

- The methods for evaluating the student's progress toward attaining his or her goals and how often the school will inform parents of this progress.

- The extent to which the student will be included in the mainstream classroom.

- The accommodations and modifications to the curriculum that the school will provide the student.

---

* The US Department of Education does offer a model IEP form at: http://idea.ed.gov/ download/modelform1_IEP.pdf. Most states post copies of their IEP forms on their department of education websites.

- The specific special education and related services that the student will receive along with their projected starting dates and duration.

- The extent of the student's participation in state and district tests, and what accommodations and modifications might be needed to allow the student to take these tests. If standard tests are not appropriate, the IEP must recommend alternative testing.

- No later than the IEP in effect on the student's 16th birthday, the IEP must list services to assist the student in making the transition from secondary school to adult life. See Chapter 11, "Transition Planning and Graduation," for more information on transition services.

- A year before the student reaches the age of majority, the IEP must contain a statement that the Team has discussed the rights that will transfer to the student at the age of majority.

TEN ESSENTIAL PARTS OF AN IEP

A long, complicated IEP can be difficult to read and understand. Failing to understand this document, however, is not an option, as otherwise parents run the risk of not knowing whether the school district is fulfilling its obligations to their child. For many years we were comforted by our son's long IEPs because they contained so much information and had so many goals. We thought this meant that he was getting the services he needed. Every year, we would study the IEP draft carefully, make revisions, suggest changes, and even meet with the director of special education to create a final version, all in the belief that it would help our son get an appropriate education. Despite all this work, our son was not able to make effective progress. We didn't understand that most of his IEP goals were so vague and unmeasurable that no one could tell if he was actually accomplishing them. We didn't realize how a lack of coordination among the information, goals, and services contributed to the document's ineffectiveness. Had we known, we would have tried harder to make sure that the goals were specific and measurable, and that the services were coordinated appropriately with the goals.

While we can't describe the IEP as each state defines it, we have learned that there are certain parts that require special attention. These parts contain the information that is most prone to misunderstanding by parents or are susceptible to the "school rules" that make the IEP less effective. Note that the following topics don't cover every part of an IEP, nor is every part we describe required by IDEA, though many state IEP forms include them. For a more comprehensive overview of all the parts of an IEP, we recommend many helpful books and websites in Appendix C.

Parent and/or student concerns

Although not required by IDEA, all the IEPs we have seen contain a place for parents and the student, if old enough, to write about the concerns they want to see addressed in the coming year. Examples of concerns might be: "Parents would like to see student improve math skills," or "Student would like to learn better self-advocacy skills." Compose your concerns carefully and thoughtfully, because they provide important information that the Team may need to develop goals and consider services that will address these concerns. Since the section on parental concerns belongs exclusively to parents, school personnel should not write this section, edit it, or condense what you write. A clear and concise statement of concerns is invaluable for developing an accurate picture of the whole student, without which the IEP can't fully address his or her unique needs.

Testing results

The IEP should list the results of any assessment the student has taken, such as the Woodcock-Johnson Tests of Achievement and Cognitive Ability, Gates-MacGinitie Reading Test, or state standardized tests. Even though this data may be part of the student's evaluations, the evaluations aren't usually available to the people who are implementing the IEP. It is helpful to specify the grade level of each testing area, such as "Written Expression 6.2 G.L." Knowing if a student is at, below, or above grade level is useful information for teachers and school specialists to help them better understand the student's needs. If an IEP makes no mention of the student's evaluation results, that will make it harder for the Team to write effective goals or the special education staff to provide appropriate services.

Student's disability and diagnosis

After listing pertinent testing results, the IEP should contain a description of the student's disability(ies). The description should be as specific as possible, with a current diagnosis by a qualified evaluator. We have noticed that there is a tendency in the IEPs we have reviewed to list only broad categories of disability, such as "health," "neurological," or "emotional," without adding essential details, such as "language-based learning disability" or a specific disability in reading or math. Some IEPs don't mention a disability or diagnosis at all.

Although the inclusion of a diagnosis isn't required by law and some parents may be uncomfortable having one written in, we have found that if an IEP lacks a complete and accurate diagnosis, it can affect the services a student receives. In elementary school our son tested with a disability in written expression and difficulty with fine motor skills. The information about his writing disability never appeared in his IEP, and as a result the Team recommended only occupational therapy to correct his grip holding a pencil. The more important issue of his written expression disability, which should have been addressed by a speech and language pathologist, was not mentioned and he never received the appropriate therapy to correct it. By the time he left the public school at the end of eighth grade, he was several years below grade level in writing. The lesson is that a missing diagnosis or overly broad categories describing a disability may result in the student not getting the specialized instruction he or she needs.

Present levels of performance

IDEA-04 requires that an IEP contain a description of a student's "present levels of academic achievement and functional performance,"[53] generally known by the acronym PLEP,* although some professionals use the acronyms PLOP or the tongue twisting PLAAFP. The PLEP describes how the student's disability impacts his or her overall progress in academic as well as in social–emotional and behavioral areas. Having this information helps the Team identify the appropriate types of instruction and accommodations needed for the student to make effective progress.

---

* The acronym comes from the language in IDEA-97, which specified that the IEP include a statement of the student's "present levels of educational performance." While the language in IDEA-04 changed to include both academic and functional performance, most people still use the old acronym.

In describing the general academic curriculum, the PLEP should indicate which specific subject areas, such as English Language Arts, Sciences and Technology, Mathematics, or Social Studies, are affected by the student's disability. For each area there should be a description of the student's current performance in the classroom, such as a listing of recent grades or a summary of the student's classroom behavior, e.g., "He does not complete homework consistently and assignments are handed in late, or not at all." The purpose is to indicate how the student's disability affects progress in the subject area. For non-academic performance, the PLEP serves the same purpose in describing how the student's disability affects areas such as social–emotional, adapted physical education, behavior, or extra-curricular activities. The PLEP should include details on specialized instruction, methodology, modifications, and accommodations the student needs to receive in each area.

It is important that the PLEP reflects the available testing data and diagnosis, and describes how a student's performance can be objectively analyzed. We have seen many IEPs use only subjective methods, like teacher observations, for determining current student performance, even when testing data was readily available. While classroom observation is important, the PLEP should not rely on it exclusively.

Vision statement

Another section that isn't required by federal law but is by many states, the vision statement is one of the most important and overlooked parts of the IEP. The vision statement is a collaborative effort between the parents and the other Team members that describes what the Team hopes a student will be doing in the next one to five years. Articulating a vision for the future helps the Team consider not only the current school year, but the upcoming ones through graduation and beyond. If old enough, a student can add his or her input to the vision statement. When the Team understands a student's aspirations, it can write better goals to help that student achieve them.

Putting some serious thought into what you want your child to achieve in the next one to five years is a valuable exercise, because it encourages thinking about the future. Frequently, parents of children with special needs are completely caught up in the moment, unable to get past their current challenges. Thinking ahead five years or even one year can seem impossible. Yet, it is important because the school's Team members are primarily focused on short-term goals, usually no longer than a school year. It is you who must consider long-range goals since you know your child's interests and preferences better than the school, and have a greater stake in your child's future prospects. Consider that Teams usually last for nine months at a time, which encourages thinking about a student for only a school year. The vision statement is what guides Teams to programs and goals that will help a student throughout his or her remaining school years and ultimately in life after high school.

VAGUE AND BRIEF VS. SPECIFIC AND DETAILED VISION STATEMENTS

In composing your thoughts about the vision statement, consider your child's abilities, not disabilities. Always have high expectations, because if you don't, the Team may not either. Make your input to the vision statement as specific as you can. Mention details, such as your child's preferences and interests, so other members of the Team can see the whole picture. Rather than refer to vague future goals, clarify what they are. By age 16, the vision statement should also include what the student aspires to after graduation, such as attending college, receiving vocational training, or living independently.

We have read many vague and brief vision statements that need further details and clarification. These actual examples will give you an idea of what to avoid:

> [Student's]* Team sees her having a smooth transition to High School. They would like her to gain the skills necessary to move on to college.

> Parents would like to see [student] continue to get the support she needs. She is a motivated student and they feel she can reach future goals with the supports in place.

> The Team hopes that [student] will successfully complete his goals and make progress both socially and academically.

What's wrong with these? The first two sound good, but lack details. The third, in addition to lacking specificity, contains circular logic. Since

---

*   As in other chapters, when we quote from actual documents, [student] replaces the student's name.

vision statements are supposed to guide the Team in formulating goals, how helpful is it to have a vision statement that "hopes" a student will complete his goals? All these vision statements would be more effective if they contained specific descriptions of post-secondary education or work-related goals. They should also include the outcomes that you and your child would like to see for the future, such as experiences in the community, economic independence, acquiring a driver's license, or independent living. An appropriate vision statement written by a hypothetical high school student might read like this:

> I would like to take high school courses that prepare me for applying to a four-year residential college. With the proper supports, I feel I can attend a competitive college, and would like to work with my high school guidance counselor each year to plan my course of study for this goal. I want to find a part-time job or volunteer work so I can participate in the community. I would also like to get my driver's license so I can travel independently. In high school, I would like to become a better advocate for myself so I can ask for what I need in order to be successful.

For an elementary school student, parents and other Team members might write a vision statement like this:

> For grade three, we expect [student] to be reading and writing at grade level as measured by testing in the spring. We expect that he will receive the necessary support and specialized instruction to do this. We want him to achieve his potential academically so that he is at grade level every year through elementary school.

Remember that as the Team revises the IEP each year, you will need to update the vision statement. Adjust it to match your own hopes for a younger child or the expressed hopes and vision of an older child. Keep in mind that the ultimate goal for all students is to live independently and productively.

IEP goals

According to IDEA, the IEP must set forth goals for the student that are objective and measurable. Once a student has mastered a goal, then the Team can write a new goal. Most IEP forms reserve a page for each goal, including the student's current level of performance in the area of the goal. The most important thing you can do is make sure that the IEP contains specific, time-limited, and measurable goals that are realistic for your child. If the goals are too easy, that is not helpful. If the goals are unattainable, that is frustrating.

CURRENT LEVEL OF PERFORMANCE

Where the PLEP describes how a disability affects a student's overall academic and non-academic performance, each IEP goal should be preceded by a description of the student's current ability in the specific skill area covered by that goal. Simply put, if you want to create a realistic and attainable goal for a skill, you first have to know the student's starting point. Knowing how far a student is below grade level, for example, helps answer the questions about what kind of specialized instruction is needed and how intensively it should be given. A student who is three years below grade level in math will need more intensive math instruction than one who is only a year below grade level.

The most effective way to determine the current level of performance is through testing data. In reading, the Woodcock-Johnson Test or Wechsler Individual Achievement Test (WIAT) is considered a good indicator of current performance. In non-academic areas, a psychological evaluation can indicate social–emotional or behavioral performance, and a test of fine or gross motor skills can indicate occupational or physical therapy performance. More general assessment methods, such as the completion of a reading skills class or participation in a sports activity, can be helpful, but there is a definite relationship between the quality of the assessment and the quality of the goal. We have noticed that the less objective the assessment, the more vague and ineffective the goal. In IEPs where the current level of performance for a skill is simply an anecdotal description of behavior without any objective data to back it up, the resulting goal is often so vague that there is little, if any, chance of the student achieving it. We give actual examples of many vague and hard-to-measure goals in Chapter 7, "Writing Effective IEP Goals." In almost every case these goals were preceded by performance assessments that were equally vague.

MEASURING PROGRESS

Every IEP goal should contain a standardized and objective way to measure the student's progress toward reaching it. How, for example, can you measure progress toward one of our son's seventh grade goals:

"[Student] will demonstrate skills in relaxing to reduce body and mental tension"? It is still hard for us to accept that we didn't question this goal at the time.

You and your Team must collaborate on setting realistic goals that require concrete, objective proof of achievement. Writing these types of goals and how to measure progress toward attaining them is such an important topic that we devote the entire next chapter to explaining these points in greater detail.

Service delivery

The model IEP form provides a chart, or "grid," that lists the services the school will provide to help the student reach his or her IEP goals. These include both direct services to the student and consultation for school personnel and/or parents (indirect services). Under the 2004 revision of IDEA, schools are directed to provide services based on "peer-reviewed research to the extent practicable."[54] If these services are not clearly described in the grid, ask what they are and have that information added to the IEP.

No matter how well written the goals are, without adequate services a student cannot receive an appropriate education, as we discovered in elementary school. Even as our son struggled to learn basic reading skills, his specialized reading instruction was limited to only 30 minutes a day. As a result, he did not become a fluent reader until fourth grade, by which time he was behind in every academic area that required reading. This problem was not isolated to his reading instruction; it extended to other areas such as math and written composition. Although on paper the number of services listed for all his goals looked impressive, their frequency and duration were minimal. Because service delivery determines how effective IEP goals can be, this is also discussed in greater detail in the next chapter.

Team determination of educational placement

Only after deciding on goals and services should the Team propose a placement for the student. Placement is the term for the location where the student will receive his or her education and how much of the school day will include specialized services. By law, a student is entitled to placement in an appropriate setting, without regard to the cost.* Parents can either accept the Team's placement decision or reject it, so make sure you understand what the school district is offering. Placement is often a source of conflict between schools and parents. If this conflict can't be resolved by any other means, you may have to resort to mediation or a due process hearing, topics discussed in Chapter 10, "The Legal Process."

Transition services

A transition service is one designed to help a student on an IEP make the move from high school to adult life, whether the transition is to college, vocational training, or independent living. To facilitate the transition, the IEP should list a student's post-secondary goals by the time the student reaches age 16. This section should include details such as the anticipated graduation date from high school, a statement of interagency responsibilities (i.e., what agency, if any, takes over from the school district), and a discussion of any guardianship issues, if necessary. Check your state department of education's website to learn what services are available for students after they graduate. Chapter 11, "Transition Planning and Graduation," contains a more detailed discussion of these topics.

Parent's Response to the IEP

Toward the end of most IEPs is a page for parents to respond to the completed document. Parents have the choice of accepting the IEP as developed, rejecting it completely, or rejecting specific parts of it. This page is where you can describe any parts you reject. In many states, you can also request a meeting to discuss the portions you have rejected.

At the bottom of the response page is a place for the parent or guardian's signature and, if the student is 18 or older, the student's signature. IDEA does not require a parent to sign the IEP, but many states require that both the school district and parents (or adult student) sign each IEP before it takes the force of a legal contract. Depending on the state, if parents do not sign and return the IEP, then either the old IEP remains in effect or the new IEP is implemented without the

---

* For more information about placement, see the section "A Closer Look at the Law" in Chapter 1, "Getting Started in Special Education."

parent's signature. Check to see what your state requires. In all cases, it is prudent for parents and representatives of the school district to sign, as the IEP is a legally enforceable contract and signatures provide a record of who has agreed to what. In case you decide at a later date that you want to reject either the entire IEP or parts of it, you can revoke your consent at any time.[55]

WHAT PARENTS CAN DO

Here is a list of suggestions on how you can use the information in this chapter:

- Know the difference between an IEP and a 504 Plan, and carefully consider which will best help your child. If the school offers your child a 504 Plan instead of an IEP, do not rely on assurances, even written ones, that your child will receive appropriate individualized instruction. Under Section 504 you have fewer rights and safeguards than under IDEA, and in some states schools can withdraw agreed-upon accommodations at any time.

- Discuss the most important aspects of an IEP with the people who are responsible for implementing them. It is the ability to implement an IEP that helps the student; otherwise even the best plan is worth nothing. Be prepared to give your child's teachers and service providers a full copy of the IEP in case the school has not provided them with one. Teachers in middle and high school may be more resistant to meeting with parents than elementary school teachers, so you should get approval from your liaison or the school administration before asking for a meeting.

- If at all possible, involve an older student in the development of his or her own IEP, especially the student concerns and vision statement sections. You will have to judge when your child is ready for this, but many high school students are able to attend IEP meetings, even if just for a short while. By the age of majority in your state, a student can sign his or her own IEP, so prepare the student for this ahead of time.

- Make sure that the IEP contains an accurate description of your child's disability(ies) and, if you are comfortable including it, the current diagnosis. If necessary, update this information each year during the annual IEP review.

- Before writing a goal, make sure that you and the rest of the Team have a good understanding of your child's current level of performance in the skill being addressed by that goal. The best descriptions of performance come from objective data found in the most recent evaluations. While anecdotal descriptions can be useful to supplement testing data, do not rely on them exclusively.

- Ask your Team what research-based methodology will be included in the IEP for teaching your child. If you have testing data that supports it, have an outside, independent professional attend a Team meeting to discuss and make a recommendation for a particular methodology.

- Never sign an IEP until you completely read it and fully understand its contents. If school personnel ask you to sign a copy at the end of an IEP meeting, politely say "No" so that you will have time to fully review it. You will have approximately 30 days (depending on your state) to consider your options before returning the final document. Once you approve the contents, or include a statement describing any sections you reject, be sure to sign the IEP, as this creates a legal record of what you have or have not agreed to.

CHAPTER 7

WRITING EFFECTIVE IEP GOALS

IEPs too often contain goals that are not specific and measurable. "Measurable" in this case means that the end result should be something that can be objectively measured within a certain, realistic time period. An example of a measurable goal might be that a student will "improve keyboarding skills to 50 words a minute by June." When goals are vague and contain only subjective methods for measuring progress, it becomes difficult, even impossible, to know if a student is actually receiving any benefit from the services he or she is getting. For years, from elementary school through middle school, our son's IEP contained goals that never changed, in part because the goals were so vague that there was no way to know if they had been accomplished. This kept us from knowing what actual progress he was making and prevented the Team from formulating progressively more advanced goals. Yet, at the time the goals sounded good to us.

IDEA clearly states that IEP goals must be measurable. Put another way, vague and unmeasurable goals are against the law. Both parents and educators need to understand this important point.Unfortunately, we have found that it is usually up to the parents to insist upon this basic right and to assist Teams in writing effective and measurable goals. If a student's progress cannot be objectively measured, then it is possible that the student is not getting the free and appropriate education mandated by IDEA.

VAGUE GOALS VS. SPECIFIC GOALS

Vague goals, like "[Student]* will increase his homework production," "demonstrate appropriate behavior in the classroom," "increase her

---

* These are goals we have found in actual IEPs. As in other chapters, names are replaced by [student] and in a few cases bad grammar has been corrected. Otherwise, the quotes are verbatim.

study skill techniques," "reflect on situations when they occur," or "demonstrate adaptive behaviors," don't indicate how the result will be measured, who will assist the student in accomplishing the goal, or how anyone will know when the goal has been achieved. Even though these goals may sound good, at the end of the year there will be no concrete evidence to indicate whether they have been accomplished. With no objective standard for measurement there may even be the temptation to think that a goal has been partially or even fully met, when in fact the opposite might be true. While IDEA requires that all IEP goals include standards for measuring a student's progress, we believe that to be effective, IEP goals should also specify the following information:

- the type of services a student needs to achieve that goal

- the dates that services begin and end

- where and how often the services are provided to the student

- who is responsible for providing the services.

Although this information should also be included in the service delivery grid (see the section "Coordinating goals with the service delivery grid" later in this chapter), the duplication reminds both the Team and the service providers that any success the student might have in achieving the goal depends on these factors.

Measurability of goals

There are four characteristics of a measurable goal:[56]

1. It contains a method for measuring whether or not the goal has been achieved.

2. The criteria for measuring progress are clearly defined in the goal and do not require any information other than what is contained in the description of the goal.

3. The measurement can be validated by multiple observers. For example, if two different observers measure the progress of a goal using the criteria described in the goal, they would independently come to the same conclusion.

4. It is possible to determine how much progress a student has made toward attaining the goal at any time, such as in a quarterly report.

Many of the IEP goals we have seen provide little of this information. Most are impossibly vague, contain no standards by which anyone could determine if the goal was ever achieved, and perversely, often place the responsibility for achieving the goal completely on the student.

ACTUAL IEP GOALS AND HOW THEY SHOULD HAVE BEEN WRITTEN

We have seen our share of poorly written IEP goals and the problems they create. The following goals and accompanying benchmarks* were actually written for various students in our state. Following each goal we describe what is wrong with it and suggest how it might be written more effectively. In general, the problems these goals share can be grouped into three categories:

- goals containing no measurement criteria

- goals that place all the responsibility for progress on the student

- goals that try to solve too many problems at once.

No measurement criteria

The primary problem with many IEP goals is that they lack any objective measurement to determine whether the goal is achieved. Sometimes this can be hard to spot. For example, we have seen goals that include impressive-sounding numbers that really don't measure anything, such as one that read: "[Student] will talk directly with adults about his behavior and academic responsibilities 80% of the time." Illustrating this problem are the following goals for self-confidence and assertive behavior that we found in an IEP for a student in the third grade:

---

* Although IDEA-04 eliminated the requirement for Benchmarks/Objectives for most IEPs, our state continues to require them.

Measurable Annual Goal: [Student] will increase self-confidence.

Benchmarks/Objectives:

> [Student] will explore and recognize his strengths.

> [Student] will utilize his strengths to accomplish tasks.

Evaluation: Observation by classroom teacher, resource room teacher, guidance counselor, and parents.

Measurable Annual Goal: [Student] will learn assertive behavior.

Benchmarks/Objectives:

> Given the classroom setting, [student] will continue to demonstrate the ability to offer help and/or positive comments to peers about his work or behavior.

Evaluation: Observation by classroom teacher, resource room teacher, guidance counselor, and parents.

WHAT'S WRONG WITH THESE GOALS

Both goals are subjective. There is no specified method to objectively measure the student's self-confidence or assertive behavior (if those qualities can be objectively measured at all), and there is no mention of what tasks the student is expected to accomplish in the first goal. In addition, both goals require a third grade student to do everything all by himself. There is no mention in the goals of who will help the student and when. Finally, if the evaluation is going to be by observation in the classroom setting, what role are the parents supposed to play in the evaluation process?

HOW THESE GOALS SHOULD HAVE BEEN WRITTEN

The Team needs to define the specific behaviors it is looking for. What are the situations that may cause the student to feel timid and lack confidence? What are the student's strengths that he can use to help him achieve these goals? This information can be provided in a description of the student's current level of performance. In addition, there must be objective criteria that will demonstrate an improvement in the behavior. Consider the following rewrite:

Measurable Annual Goal: [Student] will increase self-confidence.

With the help of the guidance counselor, in private sessions once a week for 30 minutes, [student] will explore and recognize his strengths. In these sessions, [student] and guidance counselor will identify and make a list of ways to utilize his strengths to overcome his reluctance to join in games at recess and socialize with friends at lunch. They will identify the situations that cause [student] to feel timid and list the ways [student] can feel more comfortable.

Evaluation: By the end of the school year, [student] will join in a game with others twice a week at recess. During lunch, [student] will eat with at least one friend three times a week. Observation by classroom teacher, resource room teacher, and guidance counselor. Written feedback to parents on a monthly basis.

Measurable Annual Goal: [student] will learn assertive behavior.

With the help of the guidance counselor, in private sessions once a week for 30 minutes, [student] will learn how to offer help and positive comments to peers about their work or behavior. The guidance counselor will also include [student] in a small group session to practice these skills once a week.

Evaluation: Guidance counselor will observe the number of positive interactions [student] has with peers in group sessions. By the end of the year, [student] will have twice as many positive interactions in a session as when the sessions started. Written feedback to parents on a monthly basis.

Placing the responsibility on the student

Another common problem we have observed is placing the burden of achieving a goal on the student. Why, if students need no help in accomplishing a goal, do they need an IEP? Yet this doesn't seem to stop some Teams from writing IEP goals as if a student had no special needs at all. Illustrating this problem is the following goal for written language that we found in an IEP for a student in the seventh grade:

Measurable Annual Goal: [Student] will explore various technologies to assist his writing output.

Benchmarks/Objectives:

> [Student] will investigate and use computer programs that assist him with the organization of his writing, as measured by teacher observations.

> [Student] will experiment with voice activated technology to discover whether it can be a strategy to assist him with his writing, as measured by teacher observations.

What's wrong with this goal

"Student will explore various technologies" is, of course, too vague to ever be measured. More troubling is the fact that the goal places all the effort on the student. He is the one who will "investigate" and "experiment"; the teacher (is it the classroom teacher or a resource room teacher?) will only observe. Even though the benchmark mentions that the teacher will "measure" the student's use of the computer programs, there is no mention of what is being measured or how that measurement will reveal when the student's goal is achieved.

How this goal should have been written

To make this an effective goal, there first needs to be a clear description of the student's current level of performance in writing ability (see the section "Current Level of Performance" in the previous chapter for the importance of this information and how it should be measured). This will help the Team determine how the student will achieve the goal and how the school will measure the student's progress. More important is what resources, other than providing the "computer programs" and "voice activated technology," will the school offer this student to help him achieve his goal? The following rewrite illustrates how this might be accomplished:

> *Measurable Annual Goal:* [Student] will improve his ability to produce a written composition.

> The speech and language pathologist will work with [student] once a week in 45-minute sessions to develop strategies for written composition to assist his writing output. With the help of the resource room teacher, [student] will use Inspiration software three times a week to develop the organization of his writing output. The resource room teacher will also instruct [student] on the use of Dragon speech recognition software to see if that is effective with [student's] writing.

Evaluation: Writing samples will be included with each quarterly progress report. By the end of the school year, [student] will be able to write a composition of at least five paragraphs. The speech and language pathologist will evaluate [student's] written composition skills using standardized tests before the end of the school year to determine if his writing is at grade level and to confirm that he has fulfilled his goal. If [student] is below grade level for writing, the speech and language pathologist will include that information in a report to parents and teachers.

These goals should be coordinated with the service delivery grid to insure that the student is spending enough time with the speech and language pathologist and the resource room teacher to make effective progress.

Trying to solve too many problems in one goal

We have seen goals that attempt to address too many issues at once. This makes it difficult, if not impossible, to determine actual progress, because a student may be successful with one part of the goal but not others. Illustrating this problem is the following goal with a specific focus on school behavior found in an IEP for a student in the 11th grade:

Measurable Annual Goal: [Student] will continue to take responsibility for his school work and his behavior in the school setting.

Benchmarks / Objectives:

[Student] will follow his class and work schedule on a daily basis.

[Student] will keep appropriate personal space between himself and others, i.e., not touching others, avoiding getting so close that people are uncomfortable.

[Student] will ask only appropriate questions and make only appropriate comments relating to classroom activities when in a classroom (2 to 3 comments per class maximum).

[Student] will use appropriate language throughout the school setting.

What's wrong with this goal

This goal is trying to address academic needs, pragmatic language needs, and behavior problems all at the same time. Each problem requires a different solution and a different support person to address it. Since the student has behavior problems, the school guidance counselor or psychologist should be counseling him on a regular schedule. A speech and language pathologist is the most appropriate person to work on the areas related to pragmatic language. Academic issues are the responsibility of a special education teacher, often in conjunction with the regular education classroom teachers. As currently written, the student is completely in charge of moderating his behavior and measuring his academic progress, a sure formula for failure and a built-in excuse for the school to deny responsibility for that failure. Finally, there is no mention of who will determine if the student has achieved the goal.

How the goal should have been written

The single goal should be broken up into at least three separate goals:

Measurable Annual Goal: [Student] will maintain appropriate personal space with peers.

[Student] will meet with the school guidance counselor (or psychologist) in the counselor's office for one hour a week for counseling about his behavior.

Evaluation: By the end of the school year, classroom teachers will observe [student] maintaining an appropriate space with peers and refraining from inappropriate touching on a daily basis.

Measurable Annual Goal: [Student] will ask appropriate questions and make appropriate comments while in school.

[Student] will meet with the speech and language pathologist once a week in 30-minute sessions to identify appropriate pragmatic language in the school setting, such as the conversational hierarchy and learning how to greet others appropriately.

Evaluation: By the end of the school year, classroom teachers will observe [student] making appropriate comments, asking appropriate questions, and using appropriate language at least three times a week.

Measurable Annual Goal: [Student] will learn to follow his class and work schedule.

The resource room teacher will meet with [student] daily to discuss the timelines for his work assignments and to reinforce his class schedule. [Student] will show completed homework to the resource room teacher daily. Weekly reports to parents.

Evaluation: By the end of the school year, [student] will perform these tasks 90% of the time as recorded in weekly reports by the resource room teacher.

COORDINATING GOALS WITH THE SERVICE DELIVERY GRID

An important part of every goal is the accompanying service delivery grid. This is the part of the IEP that specifies how often a service is provided and who is working with a student to accomplish a goal. Unless the grid specifies adequate time and a properly qualified person to provide the service, it is unrealistic to expect a student to make satisfactory progress toward even the most well-written goal. Because the service delivery grid generally appears several pages after the section on goals, it is easy for parents to overlook the fact that the grid is an essential part of every IEP goal. This is why we recommend that information about who is providing services and how often also be included in the IEP goals.

We discovered that as our son advanced in the public school, the service delivery grid gradually reduced the amount of time he worked with various specialists, even though he was not making measurable progress. The fact that some goals didn't change, despite glowing progress reports, was an indication of this. As he fell farther behind in achieving his goals, the amount of time spent providing services should have increased, not decreased. The following goal illustrates this problem and is taken from the IEP of a tenth grade student:

Measurable Annual Goal: [Student] will increase his ability to complete math homework and prepare for tests.

Benchmarks / Objectives:

[Student] will consistently and accurately complete his daily math homework.

[Student] will seek additional help from math teacher at least once a month.

[Student] will consistently complete review sheets and attend review sessions prior to tests.

WHAT'S WRONG WITH THIS GOAL

Except for some vague language (how many times a week does "consistently" mean?), the goal is reasonable and the objectives are measurable. Although the measurable annual goal as written is not actually a goal but the result of attaining a goal, the objectives qualify it with some measurable items. It is reasonable to assume that the math teacher will monitor the student's homework and review sheets as well as supervise the student in review sessions. The student's grades on tests will indicate how well he has improved his ability to prepare for the tests. A close inspection of the actual service delivery grid that appears in the IEP eight pages later, however, indicates some potential problems.

Special Education and Related Services in General Education Classroom (Direct Service)				
Type of Service	Type of Personnel	Frequency and Duration/Per Cycle*	Start Date	End Date
Math	Math Teacher	2 × 15	mm/dd/yyyy	mm/dd/yyyy
Special Education and Related Services in Other Settings (Direct Service)				
Type of Service	Type of Personnel	Frequency and Duration/Per Cycle*	Start Date	End Date
Math	SPED Staff	1 × 60	mm/dd/yyyy	mm/dd/yyyy

PORTION OF ACTUAL IEP SERVICE DELIVERY GRID
RELATING TO STUDENT'S MATH GOAL.

The first problem appears in the section describing services in the General Education Classroom. The student's math teacher is allotted only two 15-minute sessions per eight-day cycle (a period slightly less than two typical school weeks) to work with the student. This is in

---

* A cycle in our district is eight school days.

the general education classroom where there are likely to be a greater number of distractions than a more structured "Other Setting" like a resource room. That's less than four minutes per day. How much can be accomplished in 15 minutes a week for a student who is struggling with math? If there were a special education support person in the classroom to give additional assistance to the student, that might make up for this lack, but the grid doesn't mention one.

Another potential problem appears in the section describing services in Other Settings, where the student is allotted one 60-minute session per eight-day cycle working with a member of the special education staff. Aside from the question of whether or not this is enough time to adequately cover the material, what are the qualifications of this staff person? Not every special education aide has the skills to tutor high school level mathematics.

We learned this when our son was in middle school and an aide was given the task of tutoring him in math, an area in which he had a documented disability. Halfway through the spring term, the aide decided that she didn't understand mathematics well enough to continue the agreed-upon one-on-one tutoring. We weren't told this and only found out with two weeks left in the term when we asked the aide in an email how the tutoring sessions were going. This was despite getting progress reports indicating that our son was on track to achieve his math goal by the end of the year.

How the goal should have been written

Because the service delivery grid appears eight pages after the student's math goals, it is easy to miss the fact that the duration of the actual services being offered is potentially inadequate and that the grid doesn't specify that a qualified person is providing math tutoring outside the classroom. To make this information unambiguously clear, we believe that either the goal or the accompanying objectives should include the minimum qualifications (not necessarily the name of a specific person) of the school staff who will provide the services indicated in the goal, how often, and for how long. There should be ample time for the services to be performed in a meaningful way. How often and for how long is something that should be fully discussed and agreed by the Team after reviewing the student's current level of performance in math. This is as important as making sure that the goal is realistic and measurable. In addition, the service delivery grid should specify a start date (ideally the beginning of the school year), and a duration (ideally until the end of the school year).

The following rewrite of the goal specifies times and the personnel providing the math tutoring. Some of this information should also go in the service delivery grid, but the redundancy helps insure that the information doesn't get overlooked.

Measurable Annual Goal: [Student] will accurately complete his daily math homework and improve his score on tests.

[Student] will meet with his math teacher at least x times a cycle for x minutes or more, and will complete review sheets and attend review sessions prior to tests. [Student] will have at least one x minute tutoring session in the resource room or other quiet, distraction-free area every cycle.

Evaluation: [Student's] math teacher will keep a log of times when [student] asks for help and attends review sessions. Copies of all graded homework and review sheets, as well as graded tests, will be available for the parents at any time and will be sent home with each quarterly report along with written feedback. [Student's] score on math tests will improve 25% by the end of the school year.

AN EXAMPLE OF A MEASURABLE IEP GOAL

Not every IEP we examined contained poorly written or thought-out goals. In some, we found goals that were both measurable and realistic. Usually these were in non-academic areas such as adapted physical education (APE) and physical therapy. The following APE goal for a student in eighth grade is a notable example:

Measurable Annual Goal: [Student] will improve object control skills by 8 percentile points, as measured by the THIGHED-2* and improve P.E. fitness testing scores 100%, as measured by the regular physical education fitness testing program.

Benchmarks/Objectives:

During formal testing with the THIGHED-2, [student] will catch a ball 2 out of 3 times by extending his arms while reaching for

---

* A test of gross motor development.

the ball when it arrives, and by catching the ball with his hands only.

[Student] will improve his fitness scores in the following categories: vertical jump score by 2 inches, shuttle run score by 2 seconds, and one mile walk/run score by 30 seconds, as measured by the regular physical education teacher.

WHAT'S RIGHT ABOUT THIS GOAL

In this situation, the adapted physical education teacher had a small group of only four students. He was able to give enough attention to each student to notice things like students repeating directions and practicing a new skill. These objectives are measurable and realistic given the small group of students who participated in this APE class. The goal also clearly states who will measure the student's progress.

IEP GOAL HALL OF SHAME

Having presented some IEP goals and described them in detail, we'd like to share some additional goals that we have seen for various students in special education. They are among the least effective and most unmeasurable goals we have read, and we imagine that certain aspects of them will sound familiar to you.

[Student] will increase the complexity with which she writes sentences, paragraphs, and papers/essays. (One of the benchmarks says she will do this with "fading assistance.")

[Student] will become more consistent in completing his required academic work.

[Student] will continue to spiral new skills and apply concepts to word problems.

[Student] will improve his consistency with written language.

[Student] will continue to maintain her independence in the high school setting.

[Student] will explore strategies to increase her problem solving success.

[Student] will demonstrate skills in relaxing to reduce body and mental tension. (One of the benchmarks says he will "use sensory diet techniques for achieving body and thought relaxation.")

[Student] will utilize specific details to improve the depth of his writing.

[Student] will consistently exhibit responsible behavior in the areas of classroom participation and assignment completion.

[Student] will work to improve the thoroughness of his daily preparation.

While it is easy to see the unintended humor in many of these goals, it is worth noting that in just about every case these statements describe what parents and students want from their special education experience. Instead of being goals, however, these statements only project the results of successfully achieving a goal and instead describe a desired outcome. These kind of "feel-good" statements appear in far too many IEPs masquerading as goals. If parents do not insist that their Teams write effective goals, then there will be no way to ever objectively measure whether or not their child is making progress toward fulfilling them.

COMPARING GOALS AND PROGRESS REPORTS

IDEA requires schools to send parents reports describing the progress a student in special education is making toward his or her IEP goals. These reports must be sent as frequently as progress reports are sent to parents of students without disabilities. Most schools do this quarterly. IEP goals and IEP progress reports should be closely linked. You should compare the progress reports with the goals each quarter and at the end of each year. Even more important, you should periodically review progress reports and goals from previous years. The reason for this is that most parents tend to focus on just the current school year. This is only natural, as parenting a child with special needs is always full of new situations and challenges. The paperwork for just one school year can be daunting enough. But taking the long view and comparing the current year's goals and progress reports to those in previous years will give you the perspective to see if the goals need updating and if the progress reports are truly accurate. If this is too much to do during the school year, reserve time for it over the summer when school isn't in session.

While our son was in the public schools, we neglected this valuable exercise, and as a result we missed some important information when it might have been useful. Years later, when we did review all his IEPs, we discovered one goal in particular that never seemed to change. Starting in second grade, his goal for written language read: "[Student] will improve his ability to translate ideas into written language." Every year in elementary school we received quarterly reports saying alternately that he was making "tremendous progress," "excellent progress," or "outstanding progress" (the phrases seemed to appear in rotation). Yet his seventh grade IEP contained, word for word, the same written language goal. Six years of "tremendous" progress and somehow he had yet to achieve this goal.

It's easy to place all the blame on the school for this failure, but there was also blame for us. We were too reassured by all the positive progress reports to question, or even notice, that the same goal kept repeating year after year and yet never seemed to be achieved. Had we taken the time to compare the current IEP goals and progress reports to previous ones at least once a year, we would have caught this problem much earlier. Ideally, we could have then worked with the Team to address the written language goal more effectively and at a younger age, when his written language problems could have been corrected more easily.

If you suspect that the school's reports don't accurately reflect your child's progress toward his or her goals, you should question the reports in writing. You can also ask an outside professional to perform an independent evaluation to see whether your child has in fact obtained the proficiency levels that the school describes. If necessary, ask for a Team meeting to discuss your concerns; you don't need to wait for the annual review meeting. If you ultimately have to file for a hearing with your state department of education, the school district can use an unchallenged report as evidence that your child was making effective progress.* For a more detailed discussion of the importance of making and keeping written records, see Chapter 9, "The Paper Trail."

---

* We have read hearing decisions in which a school district used unchallenged progress reports as part of their testimony to prove that a student was making effective progress. If the parents had disputed the inaccurate reports in writing when they felt that their child was not making progress, then they could have used this documentation to help prove their case.

WHAT PARENTS CAN DO

Here is a list of suggestions on how you can use the information in this chapter:

- Remember that the IEP is created by a Team that includes the parents. Your voice is an important part in any discussion about your child's goals. Your job is to assist the Team in developing goals that are measurable, time-limited, and specific about who is responsible for seeing that the goals are met.

- Make sure that the current performance level for each goal accurately describes what your child is capable of doing. Include the most recent testing data (including independent evaluation results) in that skill area, especially the grade level equivalent for your child's current performance.

- Have valid ways of measuring your child's progress written into every IEP goal. Include specific details for teachers to notice and to record in their observations.

- Make sure that all goals are appropriately coordinated with the service delivery grid. The grid should allow ample time for every service. Also notice who will provide the service. If no one, or just "sped staff" is listed, ask for more detail about that person's role and qualifications. Pay attention to the location, start, and end dates of the service.

- Carefully read IEP progress reports and compare them to your child's actual performance. If you believe that your child is not making progress when the progress reports claim that he or she is, express your concerns in writing to your special education liaison and director of special education. If necessary, ask for a Team meeting to discuss this. Do not be lulled by lavish praise. Praise is nice to hear, but make sure there is objective data to back it up.

- Once a year, compare last year's IEP and progress reports to this year's IEP and progress reports to make sure the goals are appropriate and that your child is making real progress. If the same goal keeps appearing, it means that your child is not making progress. It is also good to compare IEPs over several years.

CHAPTER 8

TEAM MEETINGS

Team meetings are a major part of the special education experience. Once your child enters special education, a Team composed of you, a special education liaison, teachers, specialists, and sometimes administrators, will meet periodically to discuss many important issues, such as evaluations, your child's strengths and weaknesses, progress toward IEP goals, services, and placement.

At a minimum, Team meetings happen once a year to review the previous year's IEP goals and develop the next year's IEP. In addition, after a qualified outside professional evaluates your child and you submit the report, the Team must consider the evaluation in any decision regarding FAPE. Some states require that the Team convene for this purpose within a specified number of days after you submit the report. Teams also meet to discuss three-year reevaluations.

GOALS OF A TEAM MEETING

Every Team meeting is different depending on the composition of the Team and the current needs of the student. In general, however, a Team meeting should have the following goals:

- To understand the student's disability and the challenges it presents toward accessing the general education curriculum.

- To develop a clear picture of the student's current abilities and expectations for future progress.

- To listen to the concerns and goals of the parents and, if appropriate, the student.

- To identify the accommodations, modifications, services, and placement the student needs to reach his or her goals during the time frame of the current IEP (usually the school year).

Not every Team meeting will explicitly address all of these goals, but it is useful to keep them in mind. Since most Team meetings have a great deal of ground to cover, staying focused on the overall goals will minimize wasted time.

TEAM MEMBERS

According to IDEA, parents and legal guardians are equal and essential participants of the Team. The school must make every effort to schedule Team meetings so that at least one parent or guardian has the opportunity to attend or participate through a conference call. Ideally, both parents or guardians should attend whenever possible. In addition to the parents or guardian, IDEA requires certain Team members, including the following:

- A required member is at least one regular education teacher who knows or will be teaching the student. This assumes that the student is (or may be) in a mainstream classroom at least part of the day

- Another required member of the Team is at least one of the student's special education teachers, or where appropriate, at least one special education service provider

- Although this person might be one of the first two Team members, IDEA requires someone knowledgeable about the availability of special education resources for the student. This might be the student's special education liaison or a special education administrator

- A final required member is a professional who can explain evaluation results and how they affect the student. The best person to do this would be the person who administered the test and wrote the report

- The student can be part of the Team if it is appropriate.[57]

Although not required, it is a good idea for school specialists who work with the student to attend, such as an occupational therapist or a school psychologist.

In addition, parents may invite anyone who knows their child and can be supportive, such as a relative, a friend, an advocate, or outside professional to their Team meetings. As a courtesy, parents should notify the school in advance of any additional people they plan to bring, though this is not required by law. The school, on the other hand, is required to provide parents with an advance written notice of who will be attending on behalf of the school. When you receive the notification, review who will attend and be sure you understand the reason for their attendance as well as the purpose of the meeting.

One insight we have developed about Team membership is that the only constant is the parents. Everyone else changes, sometimes with great frequency. No one other than you is going to be responsible for the overall well-being and success of your child. If you are not at a meeting to advocate for your child, then it is likely that no one else will.

Parents as equal participants

There is a lot of misunderstanding about the role of parents at Team meetings. IDEA requires that parents be equal participants, which many parents assume gives them an equal voice in any decisions that get made. In reality, what "equal participant" means is that schools just have to schedule meetings so that parents have the opportunity to attend and participate. Unfortunately, the difference between participant and decision maker is one that some parents may not understand.

While all members of the Team must consider the parents' concerns and review any information (such as independent evaluations) that the parents provide, IDEA is also clear about who has ultimate responsibility for making sure that a student receives an appropriate education. Since it is the school's responsibility to make sure that the IEP includes the services and placement that the student needs to attain FAPE, IDEA gives the school the final decision in these matters. If parents disagree with a Team's decision, then the only way to formally resolve that disagreement is through a mediation or a due process hearing (see Chapter 10, "The Legal Process"). If you feel that there might be a disagreement at a Team meeting over a proposed service or placement, the best solution is to come to the meeting prepared with as persuasive an argument as possible. Your goal is to get the Team to accept your point of view, or at least come to a mutually agreeable compromise, without having to resort to more drastic steps.

The role of independent professionals at Team meetings

For many reasons, the school's Team members may disagree with a parent's request for services or placement. We experienced this many times. Whatever the reason, when you feel the Team may not have the full picture of your child's needs or is not realistically addressing your concerns, you may have to go to the effort and expense of hiring a qualified outside professional to perform an independent evaluation. If the data from this evaluation supports your concerns, you can ask for a Team meeting so that the evaluator can discuss the findings and answer questions.

ADVANCE PLANNING

For Team meetings to be productive, parents must plan in advance. Time is limited for these meetings, so preparation is critical. After the initial eligibility and IEP development meetings, the general purpose of subsequent Team meetings is an annual review of the IEP, or discussion of the student's three-year reevaluations. Between the annual review and the three-year reevaluation, however, there is a wide range of possible topics that you must narrow down to the essentials.

Start by writing down your thoughts about how your child's disability affects his or her education, how your child is currently doing in school and at home, and what your concerns are for the future. If appropriate to the purpose of the meeting, you might also want to list your child's strengths, weaknesses, and interests. From this information, prepare a proposed meeting agenda that you feel covers what you want the Team to accomplish. Try to be realistic about the number of items that the Team can cover in a single meeting. Then share your list with your special education liaison a few days before the meeting. Ask to have your suggestions incorporated into the final agenda and distributed, along with your written thoughts about your child, in time for Team members to review them before the meeting. Also ask for copies of any reports or other materials that the school staff intends to discuss at the meeting so that you can review them.

When you arrive at the meeting, hand out copies of your parent report and the agreed-upon agenda to make sure that everyone has this information. This is a good way for you to document your concerns and goals for the Team. For many years, we collaborated on the Team meeting agenda with our liaison and it helped our meetings run smoothly.

MAKING TEAM MEETINGS PRODUCTIVE

Many parents feel uncomfortable at Team meetings. There are often more school personnel in the room than parents, which can leave the parents feeling outnumbered and at a disadvantage in any disagreement over goals, placement, services, or perceptions of how the student is progressing. The main topic, your child, can be an emotional one. If there are significant problems to discuss, it can be hard to focus and think clearly. It can be even harder to listen to the conversation and take notes.

You can make this situation easier if both you and your spouse or partner attend the meeting together. At the very least, never go to a Team meeting alone. If your spouse or partner is unavailable, bring a friend or relative as a note taker, because after the meeting you may not remember important points that were discussed. Having a professional advocate work with you and come to meetings is ideal, as this person should have the experience and objectivity to understand what is happening. You may also want to invite an outside professional, such as a therapist, who knows your child and can give the Team additional insight.

During a meeting, all Team members are expected to present their reports and give their input. Disrupted or unproductive Team meetings are common. During many meetings at our son's school the PA system frequently broadcast announcements, which interrupted the Team's conversations. Teachers would also leave in the middle of the meeting, citing class or other obligations. When this happens, it may be an indication that the meeting was not scheduled at an appropriate time or that the meeting agenda was unrealistic. All Team members required by IDEA must attend every meeting in its entirety unless the parent and the school agree in writing that the Team member has been excused.[58] Everyone on a Team needs to understand that without their particular point of view and input, there can't be a valid discussion of the whole student in formulating appropriate goals and recommending appropriate services.

Rushed and incomplete meetings

When a meeting is rushed and incomplete, ideally you and your liaison should schedule a second meeting to reconvene as soon as possible to complete the agenda. In practice, it is usually difficult to coordinate the schedules of all Team members on short notice and a second meeting may not happen. When a Team meeting isn't as productive as it should be, try to learn from it. Discuss what you feel still needs to be resolved with your liaison and see what ideas you can come up with to address those problems at the next meeting.

We learned this lesson during a three-year reevaluation in fourth grade. The meeting agenda included the presentation of six school evaluations, an independent neuropsychological evaluation, and development of the next year's IEP, all within a little more than an hour. It couldn't last longer than that because of everyone's schedules. Even today, our primary memory of that meeting was one of being overwhelmed and exhausted by the volume of information presented. In reviewing the written evaluations a few years later, we realized that at least two of them raised significant concerns that were never fully discussed in the meeting and were not addressed in the IEP developed from the meeting.

In hindsight, we should have understood that there was too much to cover in a single meeting and we and our liaison should have scheduled at least two separate meetings, one for the presentations and another for the IEP discussion. Unfortunately, IDEA encourages schools to consolidate reevaluation meetings with regular IEP meetings,[59] so you may have to use persuasion and logic if you want to advocate for separate meetings.

MEETING FOLLOW-UP

Just as you need to prepare for a Team meeting, you also need to do some work after the meeting. Discuss with your spouse, friend, or advocate what you think transpired at the meeting and what the outcome was. Make sure you understand what the Team agreed or disagreed on. Then follow up the meeting with a letter to your liaison to confirm your understanding of the decisions that were made at the meeting and the agreed-upon timetable for any action items. If the meeting ended before you could discuss all your concerns, mention that in your letter. Try to communicate your thoughts as soon as possible after the meeting and always keep a dated copy of your letter. This is your written record of what the Team has agreed to, which is especially important if there are action items for some Team members.

We had the experience of Team members agreeing to do something at a meeting and then doing nothing. This happened so many times that we think for some Team members saying they will do something becomes confused with thinking they have actually done it. Time goes by, what was agreed upon doesn't happen, and parents have to ask for another meeting to make the same request again. This makes the follow-up letter listing the action items and timetable essential. You can refer to this letter in future communications if the action items have not taken place within the agreed-upon time. If necessary, you can also refer to it in your response to any IEP developed at the meeting.

HOW TRUST IS LOST

Team meetings can be emotionally draining experiences, especially if there is disagreement between the school personnel and the parents. The process falls apart when parents feel that their concerns are not being acknowledged, when parents feel that school personnel are not being truthful, or when school personnel ignore or minimize documented evidence of problems. When parents believe they can no longer trust the other Team members, then the relationship between parents and school personnel suffers.

At one of our Team meetings, we submitted an independent speech and language evaluation documenting our son's longstanding disability in written language. The evaluation recommended intensive and frequent work with a speech and language pathologist. The meeting began with the district's director of special education admitting that writing had been a "profound problem" for our son throughout middle school. The school's speech and language pathologist then stated that our son did not qualify for any of her speech and language services. This opinion was based entirely on the data in the report we submitted, as she had not done her own testing, or even met our son. As she spoke, the school's speech and language pathologist made constant eye contact with the director and never looked at us the whole time. It was as if she was making sure that what she said met the approval of her employer.

As the meeting progressed, the director of special education reinforced the speech and language pathologist's view, saying that our independent speech and language pathologist had biased the testing data by giving our son "a trick question" for his writing sample. We pointed out that a recent neuropsychological exam by another independent evaluator had reached the same conclusion about our son's disability based on a completely different test. Still, both the director and the school's speech and language pathologist insisted that our son did not qualify for any speech and language services. It was an astonishing denial, especially after two outside professionals had independently confirmed his need for such services and after the director had candidly admitted at the beginning of the meeting that written language was a "profound problem" for our son.

Hidden agendas vs. open agendas

This experience made us realize how much parents are regarded as outsiders in the business of special education. School personnel who work together on a daily basis know each other and their positions in the school hierarchy intimately. They understand the unwritten school rules. Parents are rarely aware of this subtext.

This inherent tension occurs in Team meetings because there are usually two agendas happening simultaneously: parents wanting an appropriate education for their child and the school district wanting to contain costs. The stronger agenda is that of the school district. It has more people and more resources, and they present themselves as the education experts. Parents can easily believe that it is the school professionals who know best, leading parents not to question what they are told.

The school's primary concern, though, is often not the student's welfare, but the fact that special education services are expensive and the school district must pay for them. Although IDEA is clear about a student's rights, school officials watching their budgets will often come up with creative ways to deny expensive services, yet never admit that this is their agenda. The parent's agenda, on the other hand, is usually open and transparent as they talk about what they think their child needs. This can make Team meetings confusing and uncomfortable for parents, who rarely understand or even suspect the existence of these conflicting agendas.

TEAMS SAY THE DARNDEST THINGS

The conflict between what the school really wants (to save money) and what the school is supposed to do (help the student) can lead to some surprising conclusions at Team meetings. Over the years, we heard some of the most illogical, irresponsible, and contradictory statements come from the mouths of Team members.

Don't hold it against me

A memorable moment at a Team meeting occurred just before we initiated a hearing request with our state's Bureau of Special Education Appeals. The district's director of special education attended. She was grandmotherly in appearance and demeanor, but in reality was one of the toughest negotiators we have ever encountered. She started the meeting philosophically: "I know your son had a rough time in middle school, but let's let bygones be bygones." This was the person who had blocked all our efforts to obtain an appropriate placement for our son and had violated many special education laws. Now that the realization was dawning that we were about to face each other before a hearing officer, her mood suddenly softened. Apparently, she was hoping that if she was willing to forget about how the school's noncompliance with the law damaged our son's education, we would be willing to forget about it, too.

Nietzschean teaching

Another stunning absurdity was voiced by the high school's psychologist, who began a Team meeting by admitting that the school's staff wasn't always perfect: "We do make mistakes," he told us. This was the first and only time in 15 years that we ever heard such an admission. He then followed that bit of humility by immediately adding "…but the mistakes make the students stronger when they overcome them."*

A "professional's" opinion

The same school psychologist at another Team meeting was dismissive of testing data we had supplied to support an outside placement. He waved his hand over ten years of evaluations, a stack of almost 50 reports from both independent and school specialists that was several inches tall, saying simply that in his professional opinion the testing data wasn't relevant to a placement discussion. It was clear that he felt his qualifications as a high school psychologist were more substantial than the combined degrees and experience of more than a dozen other professionals. Yet, this person's qualifications were very questionable.

---

* It was the German philosopher, Friedrich Nietzsche (1844–1900), who famously wrote: "that which does not kill us makes us stronger."

This was the psychologist we describe in Chapter 2, "School Personnel," who lacked both a state license to practice psychology and a department of education certification as a school psychologist. As we discovered, he was only certified as a school guidance counselor for students in elementary and middle school through grade nine.

One thing we learned from listening to such comments is that school administrators and school personnel can make misleading and disingenuous statements at Team meetings and no one is there to hold them accountable. As long as they have the support of the district's superintendent, the only place where school personnel can be held accountable for the things they say and do is in front of a hearing officer at a due process hearing.

WHAT PARENTS CAN DO

Here is a list of suggestions on how you can use the information in this chapter:

- Prepare in advance for a Team meeting. Talk through your issues for the meeting with your spouse, partner, advocate, or trusted friend. Write down your concerns, then create a proposed agenda and share it with your special education liaison. Collaborate with that person and, if possible, create a Team agenda with the liaison. Find out what the school personnel want to discuss and try to work with them. Compiling a list of topics ahead of time is critical, since meeting time is limited and a well-prepared agenda will keep everyone focused.

- If you are unsure about how to prepare for and navigate through a Team meeting, consider hiring a professional advocate. Make sure this advocate understands the laws and will speak up on behalf of your child. An advocate won't have the emotional ties to your child that you do, and should be more objective. See Chapter 3, "Outside Professionals," for information about how to find a good advocate and what to expect from that person.

- If you have an outside professional evaluate your child, consider bringing that person to a Team meeting to explain the results of his or her evaluation and what it means for your child's education.

- Never go to a Team meeting alone. Bring at least one friend or relative who can keep notes of what is discussed and agreed to at the meeting. Don't rely on memory.

- If the meeting agenda isn't completed in the time allotted or if Team members have to leave before the end of the meeting, it indicates that the meeting wasn't scheduled at the right time or that the agenda wasn't realistic. If a follow-up meeting isn't feasible, try to work with your liaison before the next meeting to keep this problem from recurring. Always try to be realistic about the number of topics that a Team can effectively cover in a single meeting.

- Immediately after the meeting, record your thoughts and impressions. If someone took notes, get a copy of those notes. Then type a letter of understanding about what was said and agreed to at the meeting and send it to your liaison or the special education director as soon as possible. Include a list of any agreed-upon action items along with a timeline of when they will be accomplished. The letter lets the school personnel know what you expect them to do and serves as documentation for your records.

- If the school sends you a written summary of a Team meeting, review it carefully to make sure it agrees with your understanding of what was discussed and agreed to. If anything needs to be corrected or added, you should do so in writing to your liaison.

CHAPTER 9

THE PAPER TRAIL

Special education generates an enormous amount of paperwork. The longer your child is on an IEP, the more paperwork you will accumulate. It is essential that you organize and manage this paperwork. This means that in addition to your job as a parent, you now have a job as a document manager and file clerk. Take this job seriously, for without ready access to a complete history of the documents that describe your child's relationship with special education, you run the risk of missing important opportunities.

We learned this the hard way. Each year in elementary school, our son's services were gradually reduced even as he fell farther and farther behind academically. This reduction happened so slowly that it was only when we compared several years of IEPs that we noticed it. Unfortunately, our realization didn't occur until we were forced to file for a hearing with our school district and began to organize our documents chronologically. Had we been more organized earlier and known what to look for, we might have avoided the time-consuming and costly effort of seeking legal action.

WHY ORGANIZE YOUR PAPERS

You need well-organized files (your "paper trail") because there are inevitable breakdowns in communication between parents and schools. Having a clear, written record of who has said what, when it was said and to whom, serves to reduce misunderstandings and increase positive communication. It is far more likely that busy school personnel can simply forget things rather than intentionally not do them. A timely copy of a document given to the appropriate person can provide a neutral "reminder."

If a misunderstanding should escalate into a dispute, your file of documents may be the only way you can prove that something did or did not happen. If you decide to work with an advocate or a lawyer, that person can help you understand which documents are the most relevant and important. We were able to prioritize nine years of documents with the help of an advocate. Later, when it became necessary to work with a lawyer, our paper trail was well organized and we could present the most relevant documents in chronological order to show our son's history with the school district. This saved a lot of time and money in attorney's fees.

Seeing the big picture

Establishing a paper trail also gives you a method for tracking your child's progress, both academic and behavioral. Trends that develop over a period of months or even years are not always obvious at any given moment. Looking back in time through a year-by-year survey of documents can reveal important information. The big picture of your child's history is something you can share with your Team at the beginning of each school year when there are likely to be many new members who may be unfamiliar with it. Instead of simply expressing your opinion about your child's needs, you can back up your opinion with documentation.

One important exercise we did when our son was in ninth grade was to lay out all his documents, beginning with preschool, and reread them one year at a time. We saw problems that were documented in his early progress reports surfacing over and over in later reports. Certain themes emerged around these recurring problems as he became older and academic demands increased. Taking this step back and reviewing our son's full history helped us focus on his fundamental needs rather than only on the most immediate problem.

"It wasn't written down!"

These words were actually spoken to us by our director of special education toward the end of a four-hour Team meeting. Months earlier, during a telephone conversation, she had minimized our concerns about our son's lack of progress with writing assignments. The solution was simple, the director said: she would simply have our son's IEP state that he didn't need to write more than one paragraph for his writing assignments while he was in high school. Then, when he went to college, she continued, he could choose a major that didn't require any writing. Finally, once he graduated, he could work at a job that didn't require writing. In other words, her solution was to lower expectations rather than help him learn to write effectively. We were stunned by this attitude and ended the conversation. During the subsequent Team meeting, however, we mentioned that we wanted our son to become more proficient in writing. We stated that we didn't agree with the solution of minimizing expectations for high school, college, and employment instead of trying to give our son appropriate instruction. It seemed the director hadn't prepared the rest of her Team for this apparent violation of FAPE, and as the room sat in silence, the director turned to us to say, in a sharp whisper, "It wasn't written down!" The message was that since her comments were not in a written document, she did not feel responsible for them. Fortunately, we had documented this conversation in our telephone log and later in a summary letter written to the director, so there was a record of her cavalier attitude in our files.

STARTING DOWN THE TRAIL

Every document in special education is important. Even ones that seem trivial at first can be important later. You need a system for saving and organizing these documents so you don't have to undertake a major search for them later. Begin by creating a file for each school year and put all the school documents you receive into that file. Next, keep a notebook so that you can record the date, time, and a summary of any conversation you have with school personnel. Make sure each document or phone log has a full date, including the year, and if you need to make notes or underline anything, make a copy and mark the copy up. Never write on an original and never give the original to anyone, even if it is a professional evaluating your child. Only share copies. Keep the original documents in a safe place and in good condition. Even if you can do no more than this at the beginning, it is an important step to take before the papers become scattered and lost, or you forget critical conversations.

Planning for the future by organizing your documents now doesn't come naturally for most parents of children with special needs. By necessity, you are intensely focused on just managing the present, especially if there are difficulties or complications. How are you going to get through the next month or finish the school year successfully? Or, how are you going to begin the new year school year on a positive note? Remember that you are dealing with a special education bureaucracy that is capable of generating an almost unlimited amount of paper. School employees follow procedures that require sending parents a variety of documents, such as evaluations, Team meeting invitations, consent forms, IEPs, and progress reports. It can be hard to realize how important this paperwork is. It's easy to slip the latest meeting notice or consent form into a drawer filled with bills and bank statements. Some school documents can wind up in the mail basket with the clutter of catalogs and magazines. Even a recently mailed IEP can be misplaced or lost for good if your incoming mail is disorganized. Don't let this happen to you.

TYPES OF DOCUMENTS TO MANAGE

There are many different types of documents to keep track of. These include forms from the school, independent evaluations from outside professionals, notes from meetings, and logs from telephone conversations. You must manage and organize all of them. The following are some suggestions to create a workable system for paper documents, electronic communications, telephone calls, and various forms of written notes and formal letters.

Paper documents

In a file drawer or simple file box, create and label folders for your child's IEP, IEP progress reports, eligibility forms, consent forms, all school evaluations, any written logs that go back and forth between school and home with comments, and possibly samples of your child's school work. Also file copies of any standardized test scores, report cards, formal meeting notices, and pertinent medical records. Pertinent medical records are those that relate directly to your child's disability or affect your child's ability to learn.

Electronic communications

Make and file paper backup copies of all your email and other electronic communications that you write to and receive from teachers and other service providers, your special education liaison, or the school district's director of special education. Also back up the electronic files on a CD or other non-volatile media. Electronic communication is as important as all other communication. The headers and date notation can serve as proof of an agreed-upon service or notification. You may find that some schools are starting to limit email communication between teachers and parents to better control information flow.

Telephone call logs

Keep a log of telephone calls with school personnel to record what was said in the call, with whom, and when. Write down the essential facts of the conversation as soon as possible afterward. If something important was said, write a letter to that person describing what you understood in the conversation. Not having a written follow-up creates the possibility that either you or the school personnel might forget or misinterpret something that was said. Your letter can be a reminder of what was discussed, especially if it was about an action item. Your notes and letters are an important part of making sure that it happens. As we discovered many times over the years, for some people saying that they will do something is the same as believing that they have actually done it.

Meeting notes and follow-ups

Take notes at all your Team meetings. You especially want a record of everything that the Team agrees to as it relates to your child's education. If you are not good at taking notes during a meeting, have a friend or relative attend solely as a note taker. Be sure to transcribe handwritten notes as soon as possible while the specifics of the discussion are still fresh in your mind. Keep a copy of the original notes as a backup along with the transcription in your files. Then, as soon as possible after the meeting, send a letter to your liaison with a list of all the topics that were discussed and agreements that were made. This provides a record of your understanding of what happened at that meeting. If there is a misunderstanding, you can get it straightened out while memories are still fresh and it is easier to correct.

RECORDING TEAM MEETINGS

Some special education experts recommend recording Team meetings for later transcription.[60] The obvious advantage of doing this is that you have a complete and unambiguous record of what was said in the meeting that can later be submitted as evidence in a due process hearing. While that is true, we have never felt the need to record a Team meeting and instead see some potential disadvantages in doing so. Using a voice or video recorder at a meeting is likely to inhibit discussion. Team members may feel "on the record" and be less likely to talk freely about possible solutions that might benefit your child. Also, any service a Team promises in a meeting should be the primary subject of the follow-up letter to your liaison for written confirmation, which would make a transcription from a recording unnecessary.

The most significant reason, however, not to record meetings is that in our experience, when schools violate the special education laws, it is the act of the violation that is important rather than details of discussions during a meeting. When we initiated a hearing request with our school district, it was the fact that the school had not prepared an IEP for our son the previous year that was important to the hearing officer. All our other evidence, some of which was based on statements made at Team meetings, was secondary and probably wouldn't have resolved our case by itself.

What is more, IDEA does not explicitly give parents the right to record Team meetings. Some states, like California and Massachusetts, have laws requiring "all parties consent" before any recording of a conversation or a meeting can take place. This means that schools in these states have the legal right to prohibit parents from recording a Team meeting if anyone at the meeting refuses to agree to it. IDEA does require schools to give parents "the opportunity to participate"[61] so that it could be both legal and appropriate to record a Team meeting when one or both of the parents have a disability that prevents them from taking written notes, if a meeting is conducted in a language other than the parent's native tongue, or possibly even if only one parent can attend. Any school policy regarding taping must be consistent and cannot change, *ad hoc*, from family to family or from meeting to meeting.

Letters

When you write a letter to the school, either send it with a return receipt so you can prove that the school received the letter and on what date, or hand deliver it to the school's secretary with a second copy that the secretary can stamp with the current date. FAX transmission can also be useful for this purpose if you save the confirmation sheet and mail the original copy. These methods will provide proof of receipt for your files. This may sound extreme, but certain communications between parents and schools must be in writing and must be received within a certain number of days either before or after a specific event, such as unilateral placement in a school outside the district. Otherwise, you may jeopardize some due process rights.

When you receive a letter or document from the school, keep the envelope that it was mailed in with the document. The postmark date on the envelope can be important later to show whether the school complied with a specific deadline.

Parent's journal

In addition to the telephone log, it is a good idea to have another notebook handy to record your impressions of how your child is doing emotionally, socially, and academically. Write about his or her activities and other interests. Be sure to include the full date and any details you think are significant. A parent's recollections can be important to let the Team know how things are going at home and outside of school. At some point in the future, you may need this information and you cannot rely on your memory alone. We always kept our notebook in a drawer reserved for that purpose so that it was easy to find.

Canceled checks and invoices

An often-overlooked category of records is the cost of services related to special education that you pay for out of your own pocket. There are situations where having these records available will lead to full or partial reimbursement. We discovered this in negotiations about one of our disputes with our school district, when the discussion focused on the cost of the previous year's tuition at a private special education school. On another occasion, the cost of a summer program at a special needs college played an important part in a settlement discussion. In both cases, we didn't have our financial records easily available. Fortunately, these schools furnished the district with this information, so we only experienced a small delay in getting reimbursement. This was a lesson for us to keep all invoices in a file with our other special education records.

Public records

Another overlooked category of records is public information available in newspapers, magazines, or other sources. Newspaper articles that describe the public schools in your town or interviews with administrators or teachers can provide valuable background information about the attitude of your district toward the programs your school offers. We found two surveys of public school students in our town valuable in supporting our contention that the public school was not an appropriate placement for our son. One survey measured stress among middle and high school students and the other measured substance abuse in the same population. The increase in stress levels reported by students, from 30 percent in sixth grade to over 80 percent by 11th grade, matched a similar increase in reported substance abuse among those same students. While this data was not conclusive by itself, it was a strong argument that the public school environment was not a positive one for a student who had special needs and was struggling academically. Other documents, such as program reviews by state departments of education that describe compliance problems with state or federal regulations, may also be valuable as background information.

USING YOUR PAPER TRAIL

By establishing an organized history of your child's educational experience, you are creating evidence of what your child has and has not accomplished in school, and what the school district has and has not done. This will show the chronology of meetings, evaluations, conversations, requests, consent forms, IEPs, phone logs, letters, attendance sheets from meetings, and anything else that has to do with your child's educational experience. Someday you may need these documents to help tell your story to an impartial observer in a mediation or due process hearing.

You may think that a dispute that requires mediation or even a hearing will never happen to you. But if it should happen, you must be prepared. Your school district can even demand documents from you in a legal process called "discovery." We have been through this, compelled to supply the school with many of our records, and our organization was critical to doing it successfully.

One experience that taught us how important maintaining a paper trail can be came after our son's eighth-grade year when that June we failed to receive his final English progress report. The previous reports that year indicated that he had been excused from over half his written assignments, even though his IEP goals emphasized working on his writing skills. Concerned to see what the final report for the year indicated, we made several unsuccessful telephone calls that summer to the school office requesting a copy of the missing report. The next fall, we wrote a letter to the school principal about this situation. The spring progress report then quickly arrived in the mail along with an unsigned, handwritten comment stating that our son had completed all his written English assignments orally. Aside from the fact that the accommodation of doing written assignments orally was never part of his IEP, our son had no recollection of having done them in any manner.

When we later filed for a due process hearing to seek reimbursement for a private school placement, the school district's position was that our son had been making sufficient progress to enable him to achieve his annual IEP goals, including those in written composition. We were able to counter this argument by producing our son's eighth-grade English reports, which showed that he had either been excused from his written English assignments for that year or had supposedly done them orally. Our paper trail showed that the school was not providing the instruction called for in his IEP.

HOW SCHOOLS USE THEIR PAPER TRAIL

In Chapter 7, "Writing Effective IEP Goals," we described our experience with receiving consistently positive progress reports, even after it became apparent that the comments in the reports didn't match what our son was experiencing. The reason for this, we realized, was not just to make us feel better, but for the school to create its own paper trail to indicate that it was providing an appropriate education. If you take your district to a mediation or a due process hearing, the school can produce all their upbeat, positive progress reports to prove they were providing FAPE. When the progress reports you get don't match your observations and you don't dispute them in writing, the school can use them to demonstrate to a mediator or hearing officer that your child was achieving his or her IEP goals.

Schools are always prepared with written documentation to supply as evidence in a hearing. A few years ago, our school district used progress reports as part of its defense in a hearing with another family, claiming that the student's progress reports showed he was meeting the goals and objectives in his IEP. This was the school's paper trail. Throughout the 30-page hearing decision, there are seven references to the school district quoting from progress reports about how well this student was doing in the public school. This was in sharp contrast to the parents' and the experts' testimony as to how much the student was struggling and not making progress. Happily for the student and his family, there was enough other evidence for the hearing officer to rule in the family's favor.

A PARENT'S RIGHT TO INSPECT SCHOOL RECORDS

IDEA gives parents the right to inspect and make copies of their child's school records.[62] It is important to periodically examine these records, because they may contain information that you have not received. In our case, we discovered handwritten notes in the margins that we hadn't seen on the copies of documents that the school had sent us. These notes, even if they don't seem important, should be part of your files, too.

You can inspect your child's records by writing a letter to your school district requesting a convenient date and time for you to view them. Be sure to request the complete file, as documents may be in different locations—for example, medical records in the nurse's office and academic records in the special education department office. Most states have regulations that specify how much advance notice you are required to give and how quickly the school is required to respond. You can check the regulations on your state's department of education website. For a nominal copying fee, you can make copies of anything you want. If you have misplaced any documents, you should find them in your child's file and make a copy for yourself to complete your records at home. You may even find documents that you did not know existed. Going through your child's school file is a valuable exercise.

Correcting inaccurate school records

Although we have not had to do this, the Family Educational Rights and Privacy Act (FERPA) gives parents the right to ask the school to correct records that they believe are inaccurate or misleading. If the school refuses, the parents then have the right to request a hearing to compel the school to make the correction. Some state laws may give you similar or even additional rights. Of course, a hearing is an expensive and time consuming process that has no certain outcome, so it is best that you only attempt one if an error significantly impacts your child's education, and then only after you exhaust every other means to reach a mutually agreeable solution to the problem.

WHAT PARENTS CAN DO

Here is a list of suggestions on how you can use the information in this chapter:

- Start your paper trail with the following steps:

  o Create a filing system for your school documents. This should include printed copies of all electronic communications. One system that works is to have a file folder for each school year, clearly marked. If there are too many documents for one file, create as many as you need. Decide whether you want to keep the documents in chronological order or grouped by subject for that year.

  o Keep a notebook to record the date, time, and a summary of any conversation you have with school personnel.

  o Keep a journal of your impressions of your child's progress, both inside and outside school, dating each entry and including any details that you think are significant.

  o Write a letter to your special education liaison or school staff person after every Team meeting or important conversation with school personnel. Summarize your understanding of any action items or decisions that were agreed upon.

  o Get confirmation of every formal, written letter you send the school, especially those that are dependent on deadlines. Either get a return receipt, a FAX confirmation, or hand deliver the letter to the school's secretary with an extra copy that the secretary can date stamp for your records.

- Never write on the originals of important documents like IEPs and evaluations. Make copies first, then write on them. Always keep the originals in your filing system and only give copies to other professionals who might need them.

- Start to see the "big picture" of your child's education by periodically studying your child's special education documents in chronological order. Trends will become apparent as you study the details and analyze the data over time. Because Team members are transient, they don't see the overall history that parents see.

- Question progress reports if you feel they are not accurate. If you disagree with a report, write a letter to your special education liaison and point out the inaccuracies as objectively as possible. Include facts to support your position based on your own observations, your child's work, or outside testing. If the progress report is vague, write a letter asking for more specific information. By writing a letter, you have documentation for the future in case you need it. If you go to a hearing, then the hearing officer will have your letter disputing the school's reports as evidence of your child's situation.

- Periodically review your child's records at the school administrative office to be sure you have copies of everything. Look for handwritten or marginal notes that may not appear on copies of documents that you have received. Make copies of everything you don't have, and include these copies in your files.

CHAPTER 10

THE LEGAL PROCESS

Someday you may need to pursue the legal process in order to get a free and appropriate education for your child. In our case, we never imagined having to do this. We lived in an affluent town with a reputation for outstanding schools. When our son was in elementary school, we put a great deal of effort into developing a cordial relationship with school personnel. Since they told us that he was making excellent progress in all aspects of his school program, we had no major worries.

By the time our son was in middle school, the situation had changed. He was obviously not doing well, the school personnel were not so cordial, and we gradually realized that they were not acting in our son's best interests. We hired an advocate who, after studying our situation, explained to us how our district had not been compliant with the special education laws. There had been many violations over the years, even in elementary school when we thought things were going well.

With the advocate's help, we began to understand the magnitude of the problem. We then hired an attorney from a firm with experience in special education law to help us find a solution. We concluded that for our son to make effective progress, we had to remove him from the public school and place him in a private school that specialized in teaching students with learning disabilities similar to his. Taking legal action to make the school district responsible for our son's education seemed like an extreme step, but there was no other choice since our district refused to consider the less drastic step of mediation.

After years of cooperating with our Team members, getting to know them, sending them handwritten thank you notes, even baking them homemade bread at the holidays, and trying in every way possible to make the public school work, we felt betrayed. Our son had suffered and had not been able to learn to his potential. Independent testing showed that he was seriously below grade level in many areas, despite the school's claim that he was making effective progress. It was clear that we had to take action. Because time was a factor, we took the financial risk of enrolling him in a special education school and then asking the school district for reimbursement. To do this, it was necessary that we go through the legal process.

Hiring a lawyer is a delicate issue because parents must try to work cooperatively with the school at all times. Once the school personnel know you have hired an attorney, an adversarial relationship is likely to develop. For this reason, make a good faith effort to protect the relationship between your child and the people who work with him or her. When you bring a lawyer into the situation, or threaten to, this relationship can become strained. But at that point the relationship may have deteriorated anyway.

WHEN DO YOU NEED A LAWYER?

Usually, parents seek legal assistance when they have reached an impasse with their school district over what constitutes an appropriate education. If the district refuses to compromise, sometimes the only avenue left is a due process hearing. Some school districts, we have found, simply won't provide FAPE unless confronted by legal action. School administrators know that most parents of children with special needs are often exhausted, overwhelmed, and dependent on school personnel. They also understand that most parents don't know their legal rights. It is simply less expensive for them to wait until parents seek legal recourse, which they know from experience that few do. This is what we describe in the "Introduction" as the special education business plan.

Some parents become so frustrated with their school district that they make threats to hire a lawyer. If you ever feel this way, resist the temptation, as it will only make a difficult situation worse, especially if you don't actually follow through. Instead, you can hire a lawyer to work with you behind the scenes to advise you on your child's rights, whether or not you have a case, and how strong your case might be. A lawyer can guide you to prepare for a mediation or, if necessary, a due process hearing. An agreement reached during a mediation or a decision made by a hearing officer can resolve issues and help parents secure appropriate services or placement for their child.

The importance of due process rights

Perhaps the most important reason for parents to seek legal advice is to understand and protect their due process rights. These are the procedural rules that govern the legal interactions between parties. Although they may often seem trivial, these rules function as the guideposts by which parents and schools navigate the special education system. While rules aren't ends in themselves, by observing them schools show respect for parents as well as a commitment to provide FAPE. An example of what can happen when there isn't enough respect shown for due process occurred in 2011 in Massachusetts when some school districts started asking parents to sign a document they called "Procedures Lite." In this document, the districts asked parents to waive their right to IEP meetings, IEPs, progress reports, and even worse, the right to a due process hearing. Fortunately, when the Massachusetts Department of Elementary and Secondary Education found out, it "directed districts that have implemented the practice to discontinue it."[63]

Parents should not see due process as only a one-way street, however. They need to be careful not to sacrifice the goal of helping their child over disagreements about small procedural issues. The dilemma is that there is no bright line dividing the inconsequential procedural issues from the important ones. Each situation is unique. Having a clear understanding of your rights and what they mean in your particular situation is always the best guide.

FINDING THE RIGHT LAWYER

Finding a lawyer is similar to finding a doctor. You must research a candidate's credentials, find out what that person can do for you, learn the cost, and make sure he or she is a good fit. "Good fit" means someone who understands your child's disability and has a personality and style you feel comfortable with. Federal and state laws for special education can be complex, so it is also critical that a lawyer knows disability law thoroughly. Your choice of a lawyer can ultimately determine whether or not you are successful in obtaining FAPE for your child.

How does one find a lawyer? Locate and attend meetings for parents of children with special needs. There are many disability support groups, so research the groups that are active in your area or that specialize in disabilities similar to your child's. It is likely that some members of these groups will have recommendations and personal experience with lawyers. Support groups sometimes have special education professionals, including lawyers, speak at their meetings. This is a good opportunity to see an attorney demonstrate an understanding of special education law and assess how he or she interacts with parents.

You can also ask about attorneys through advocacy networks. There are several national organizations that maintain a list of resources, including special education lawyers, grouped by state. Appendix C, "Resources," lists several of these organizations. Another possibility are email groups that discuss special education issues in your area. Asking for referrals and personal experience in these groups is usually productive and a good place to gather leads. If you are working with an independent evaluator or service provider, or with an advocate, these individuals may be able to recommend an attorney. Many state department of education websites also maintain lists of legal organizations that you can contact for information and referrals.

Initial consultation

Once you have identified a lawyer you may want to use, call the law firm to discuss details with the lawyer or his or her paralegal. Should you decide to proceed, you can arrange an initial consultation and have the lawyer review some of your documents. Usually there is a fee for an in-depth assessment of your situation. This is a chance to ask if the lawyer has worked with parents in your school district and understands the special education program there. You should determine how well the lawyer understands your child's particular disability and how that understanding might affect his or her handling of your case.

Once we selected a lawyer, we met with her to review our situation and determine if we actually had a case. It is one thing to be dissatisfied with your school district, but it is another to discover that the district has violated state and federal laws. An experienced lawyer can help you sort out what has happened and advise you if there is a genuine legal recourse.

Since you will be paying for the lawyer's time, you will want to be as efficient as possible. Ask beforehand what documents to bring and how they should be organized. Write an outline of the events and possible violations of the law that you think have occurred and reference the documents that illustrate the significant points in your chronology.

After this initial consultation, a lawyer should be able to tell you if there are legal grounds for moving forward. This is the time to decide if you feel comfortable with this person and if you have the commitment and resources to go forward. If you feel there is sufficient reason to proceed, then there are a number of possibilities for the next step. Every case is unique, so there is no predictable path.

Preparing for the next step

As part of assessing your case, your attorney will want to know whether an independent professional supports the position you want to take. If you do not already have up-to-date independent evaluations, the attorney may suggest that you arrange to have such evaluations performed. In our case, once the additional evaluations were completed, we brought the evaluators to Team meetings to discuss their reports and to answer any questions that the rest of the Team had. This effort did not change the position of the school about our son's needs and proposed placement, but it was necessary to give the evaluations to the Team and place the district on notice about the evaluators' conclusions.

In addition, we met with the director of special education to try informally to resolve our situation. We started to refer to these moves as the special education chess game because we were thinking about this as part of a strategy to prove our case. We would make one move and then the school would make the next move, with us having to prove our point over and over. An ancient Chinese text actually helped us understand this process. Titled *The Art of War* by Sun Tzu, it is about using strategies, psychology, diplomacy, and calculations to prevail in a contest. This book was a great help with mental attitude, confidence, and planning our objectives.

MEDIATION

In a dispute between a school district and parents, it is possible to reach a compromise through mediation. IDEA requires that every state provide a qualified mediator at no cost to help parents and school districts reach an agreement in disputes over a child's education. Although many parents do not need a lawyer for this step, we suggest a consultation with one to decide how to present your case most effectively. The mediator does not make a judgment or a decision, but facilitates a mutually agreeable resolution. The mediator then helps the parties write an agreement and sign a legally binding document that must remain confidential and cannot be used later as evidence at a due process hearing or civil litigation.[64] Mediation is an informal, relatively quick, and inexpensive way to resolve disputes without directly using attorneys. Since participation in mediation is voluntary, both parties must agree to it before a mediation can take place. If mediation fails to resolve the dispute, both parties still have the right to proceed to a due process hearing.

DEMAND LETTER

A demand letter is a formal document requesting that another party take certain steps to rectify a situation or fulfill a contract or obligation without having to go to court. A demand letter is sometimes the first step that parents take in order to resolve problems with a school district, especially if mediation is not an option. Many school districts will respond to a demand letter if it comes from an attorney. They might be encouraged to offer a settlement in order to avoid further legal action. School districts may also ignore a demand letter, essentially daring parents to follow up with a request for a formal hearing.

Since our school district refused to consider mediation, we started with the demand letter. In this letter our lawyer described our son's educational history, his documented needs, the school's violations of the law, and the outside placement that we and our independent evaluators believed he needed to make effective progress. The school district, which we gave ten days to reply, remained silent.

DUE PROCESS HEARING

When school districts fail to respond after receiving a demand letter or when mediation and other attempts at resolution fail, the only means left to resolve a dispute is a formal request for a due process hearing. The request must be made within two years of the date that the parent knew (or should have known) about the action that forms the basis of the dispute.[65] Although it can vary from state to state, the hearing request, like the demand letter, must outline all the issues that are to be discussed in a hearing. Either the parents or the school may initiate the hearing process. Our hearing request letter described our son's educational history as well as the school district's history of violations and failure to provide FAPE. The request also outlined the relief we sought. Once our attorney sent this letter, the school's attorney became involved with our case and the school finally responded.

Resolution session

Within 15 days of parents filing a hearing request, the two parties can schedule a resolution session.[66] This is a chance for each side to discuss the dispute and understand the other side's position better. Ideally, the parties will reach an agreement. As with mediation, this is legally binding. IDEA requires a resolution session if parents file for a hearing, but not if the school district does. This is an informal opportunity to resolve the issues before bringing lawyers in; though if the parents bring an attorney, the school district may do so as well. If neither party believes that a resolution session will be productive, then the requirement to have a session may be waived and the timeline for proceeding to a hearing begins.

Pre-hearing conference

Barring a successful resolution session, the next step may be a pre-hearing conference. In this step, the parents and the school district meet with a hearing officer to identify and clarify the issues to be tried, and discuss scheduling, and other matters. Depending on the laws of your state, the hearing officer may also attempt to help the parties settle the case before it goes to a more formal hearing. In that event, both parties, their attorneys, and other persons, such as independent experts, present summaries of their cases to the hearing officer who may then give the parties an informal assessment of the strengths and weaknesses of each side's case.

While typical presentations in a pre-hearing conference may revolve around specific legal issues, we found that our hearing officer seemed especially interested in our description of our son's personal experiences. At the end of the presentations, the hearing officer raised serious questions about the actions that our school district had taken. In such a situation, many school districts would offer to compromise and settle. In our case, the school district refused to offer a settlement, so the hearing officer scheduled a four-day hearing to convene in two months. Despite clear indications that there were weaknesses in its position, the school district was going to force us to spend additional time and money.

Discovery

Discovery is a legal term for the process by which parties can request and share information before a hearing. The standards for discovery in a special education dispute vary from state to state. As a minimum IDEA requires that the parties disclose all evaluations and resulting recommendations that they intend to use at a hearing no less than five business days prior to the hearing.[67] State laws vary as to how long a party has to respond to a discovery request, but in states like ours a formal discovery process can begin once a resolution session has been held or waived, and responses are due within 30 days unless the hearing officer grants a change in the deadline. The sooner discovery is completed, the sooner a hearing can take place.

In our case, our lawyer sent a list of questions, called interrogatories, and a request for documents to the school district, and the district reciprocated with a list of questions and a document request for us. The interrogatories must be answered completely, truthfully, and under the penalty of perjury. In our discovery, we requested information on the school district's proposed placement. In return, we were asked detailed questions about why we were seeking an outside placement. Writing our answers was time-consuming, but we saw it as an opportunity to organize our thoughts and tell our story.

Receiving a discovery request can be overwhelming for parents, but it can also be an important part of due process. Some school districts use discovery as a way to intimidate parents, who may not be able or willing to answer detailed interrogatories, especially on a deadline. This can force parents to accept a lesser settlement early in the process instead of going forward with a hearing.

Motions

Prior to a hearing, both parties can file motions on a variety of issues. These are requests for the hearing officer to make a decision about a specific matter relating to the hearing. A motion can be procedural, such as asking to extend a previously set deadline, or to force a party to respond to a discovery request. A motion can also be substantive, such as asking the hearing officer for a summary disposition, which is an opinion about a single aspect of the case or even the whole case.

Exhibits

Exhibits are another part of the hearing process. They are documents you will present as evidence during the hearing. Each side must produce copies of its proposed exhibits. Many of a student's records can be used as exhibits, including IEPs, progress reports, letters to the school or from the school, report cards, school evaluations and independent evaluations, documentation about outside placements, and anything that might be relevant to your case.

If you have a well-organized paper trail (see Chapter 9), then your exhibits should be pretty much ready. These exhibits are important in explaining your case to a hearing officer who does not know you or your child. You need to present facts clearly to make your case as strong as possible. Your organizational skills will make a significant difference in explaining your child's history, situation, what remedies you are seeking, and why.

The hearing

A hearing is like a trial without a jury. It is a formal, adversarial procedure with witnesses, lawyers, testimony, cross-examination, and exhibits. In some states, a lay advocate (an advocate who is not a lawyer, but who has training in special education law) can represent parents at a hearing instead of a lawyer. Hearings are draining emotionally and financially, yet sometimes they are necessary. Parents, or the school district, can file for a hearing without a lawyer and are referred to as *pro se* parties, meaning they represent themselves. Since special education laws are complex and the hearing procedures are formal, this is not without risks. Some *pro se* parents do well at hearings, but many do not prevail. Not understanding the law and legal strategies is a disadvantage because school districts almost always bring their attorneys to hearings. If you decide to represent yourself, make sure you have a thorough understanding of the federal and state special education laws as well as an understanding of how a hearing is run.

After a hearing concludes, the hearing officer will write a decision stating the resolution of the case. This can take several weeks, depending on state law. In the decision, the hearing officer can order the school to provide services, modify the IEP, provide compensatory education, pay for placement at a private school, or require reimbursement to the parents for expenses, or whatever the hearing officer feels is necessary to obtain FAPE. The hearing officer can also rule in favor of the school district and deny these things. The hearing officer's decision is legally binding, but subject to appeal. Appealing a hearing officer's decision in court, a process that takes additional time and expense, is by no means sure to overturn the decision, however. Some states, like New York, have a process in which an appeal can first be made in a second-level administrative review before it goes to court. This can save both time and money.

Ultimately, we did not have to go through the full hearing process. Our school district finally agreed to a settlement less than two weeks before our scheduled hearing. In the meantime, we had to organize our exhibits, schedule our expert witnesses, and prepare ourselves mentally for a four-day "trial." To us, this was more evidence of the school's business plan: force the parents to spend as much time and money as possible before finally offering a fair settlement. Their cost-based calculation is that most parents will give up or accept a lower settlement amount before this happens.

Stay put

One of the safeguards written into IDEA is the right to placement pending appeal, commonly known as "stay put."[68] Stay put means that the school cannot remove services from or change the placement of a student while the issue of those services or placement is under dispute. This is an important right for parents, since it can often take many months from the time they make a hearing request until an issue is resolved. All this time the district can't change the student's status over the parents' objections. In this situation, stay put insures that there is no disruption in the student's education while the parents and the school district resolve their disagreement. Of course, parents always have the option to change a student's placement at their own risk, as we did when we unilaterally placed our son in a private special education school.

Research and think twice

Before having your lawyer file a hearing request, you should read some actual decisions written by hearing officers in your state to see what hearings are like. In our state, the department of education website makes hearing decisions available with the names of the students and parents redacted. Most other states offer a similar service; you should check your state's department of education website. Also, many special education law firms' websites or blogs post commentaries on hearing decisions in their area. Reading actual decisions and legal commentaries will give you an idea as to what worked for parents and what didn't. The law firm of Kotin, Crabtree & Strong (www.kcslegal.com), for example, posts commentaries on many recent hearing decisions in Massachusetts.

If everything we have described hasn't made you think twice about initiating a due process hearing, one additional thought to consider is that, although the district may be required to reimburse you for attorney's fees if you ultimately prevail, you may be ordered to reimburse your school district for their legal fees if a court determines that you have filed a hearing request for improper reasons. These reasons include trying to cause an unnecessary delay, filing for frivolous reasons, trying to harass the school district, or filing for a hearing without evidence.*

It is worth reflecting on the fact that taking your school district to a hearing is not a goal, even if it may ultimately be necessary. The true goal is to find the most cost- and time-effective way to get your child FAPE. So proceed carefully with solid advice from an experienced professional. As Sun Tzu wrote 2500 years ago: "It is best to win without fighting."[70]

SETTLEMENT AGREEMENTS AND CONFIDENTIALITY

If you reach an agreement, the parties will create a document that spells out all the terms of the agreement. We strongly encourage parents to have their own lawyer write the agreement, not the school's lawyer. If the school's lawyer does prepare the first draft, you and your

---

* This does not mean that schools can shift fees to the parents if the parents merely lose their case. The courts have decided that the case must be "so lacking in arguable merit as to be groundless…"[69]

attorney must review it carefully. The aphorism "The devil is in the details" applies to this document and you need to make sure the terms are actually what you have agreed to. There is no room for error or sloppiness.

One item that is frequently included in a settlement agreement is the confidentiality provision, or "gag order." This is a paragraph specifying that the parties involved must keep the "facts or terms" of the settlement confidential. Typically, the gag order allows parties to make only the following statement: "The underlying dispute in this case has been resolved in a manner satisfactory to all parties." Though it has little or no benefit for parents, the gag order serves the school in two ways. First, it prevents other parents of students in special education from finding out that the school has been forced to provide FAPE so that they might be encouraged to seek the same remedy. Second, it keeps the town's residents from learning that the school has been forced to settle with parents for what may be large sums of their tax dollars. Thus, gag orders are popular with school administrators.

In our case, the school district did not initially ask for a gag order. After our lawyer wrote the settlement agreement without a confidentiality clause and had it approved by the school's representative, we signed the document and hand delivered it to the director of special education, who signed it a few days later. Only after that did the school notice that there was no gag order in the signed agreement and asked us to sign one. Since confidentiality had not been requested during negotiations, and since the settlement had already been agreed to and signed by all parties, we refused on principle.

WHAT PARENTS CAN DO

Here is a list of suggestions on how you can use the information in this chapter:

- Only consider a due process hearing as a last resort. First, do everything you can to resolve disputes with your school district informally. If you do have to pursue a hearing, the hearing officer will want to know that you made every effort to resolve your issues before entering the legal process.

- Hiring a lawyer begins an adversarial relationship with the school, so you may want to be discreet at first and have your lawyer advise you behind the scenes. Once you signal that you have a lawyer, then your relationship with the school will change. Never threaten to hire a lawyer, even if you mean it. You may risk increasing any adversarial relationship with the school and possibly weakening your case, especially if you don't follow through.

- Make sure you have a strong case before proceeding with a hearing request. An initial consultation with a special education attorney can establish if it is worth going forward legally.

- If necessary, be prepared to remind the school, in writing, of IDEA's "stay put" requirement if you are disputing a change in services or placement. This will maintain the continuity of your child's education while you resolve these issues.

- Be sure of your determination, fortitude, and financial resources before undertaking a due process hearing. School districts know that legal action is a difficult and expensive process for parents and some will attempt as many delays and calculated postponements as possible to wear parents out before going to a hearing.

- Even if you know that you are heading toward a hearing, cooperate fully with the school. Schedule and attend the required Team meetings to discuss evaluations, IEPs, placements, and other details in your case. The hearing officer will want to know that you have brought all relevant facts to the district's attention and that you have followed the Team process.

- If your district proposes a gag order as part of a settlement, you can object. If the district insists, you will have to decide whether it is worth agreeing to it in order to achieve the other terms you have agreed to in the settlement.

CHAPTER 11

TRANSITION PLANNING AND GRADUATION

Graduation is usually a time of celebration, when young people complete their high school studies and move on to work or college. For parents of students on IEPs, graduation has an additional significance because it ends their child's right to special education. While IDEA makes it possible for students to receive special education services through the age of 21* to help them prepare for the future, once a student accepts a high school diploma these services end regardless of age. This makes planning for the transition to adult life and graduation closely linked. Transition planning needs to occur first, followed by transition services, and only then by graduation. The goal is not to graduate on a schedule, but for the student to become a productive member of society and function independently in adult life.

WHY PLANNING IS IMPORTANT

The President's Commission on Excellence in Special Education warned in 2002: "Too few [children with disabilities] successfully graduate from high school or transition to full employment and post-secondary opportunities, despite provisions in IDEA providing for transition services."[72] Ten years later, in 2012, the Government Accountability Office reported that "students with disabilities are less likely than their peers to successfully make the transition [to the workforce]," and that "the employment rate for young adults ages 20 to 24 with disabilities was less than half the rate of their peers

---

*   The actual end date for special education services depends on state law and can vary between the age of 18 through the age of 21. Our state, for example, requires special education services for students on an IEP until their 22nd birthday, or the acceptance of a standard high school diploma, whichever comes first.[71] You should check to see what your state requires.

without disabilities." The GAO report pointed to the primary causes of this problem:

- Parents and students don't receive enough information about the full range of available transition services after high school.

- Programs providing transition services are not always coordinated and are difficult for students to navigate.

- Students with disabilities graduate from high school without being well prepared for post-secondary education or employment.[73]

In other words, the last decade has produced little or no progress in the prospects for students with disabilities in either higher education or employment. Without thoughtful transition planning, this situation is unlikely to change.

TRANSITION PLANNING AND SERVICES

Transition planning and transition services are important steps toward achieving independence. IDEA requires these, because otherwise students with disabilities might "languish at home, their ability to become independent and self-sufficient (therefore making a positive contribution to society) placed at significant risk."[74] If this were to happen, it would mean that years of special education effort and expense would be wasted and increase the risk that these individuals could become dependent on welfare and social services. Transition services are a small investment compared to the cost to society of supporting a dependent person for their entire adult life.

For this reason, IDEA requires that the IEP in effect when the student turns 16 must contain a written plan to help a student make the transition to adult life.[75] The plan should outline a course of study and specify the services needed to support a successful transition, including identification of any possible state agencies outside the school district responsible for helping with the transition.

Transition planning means more than just planning for academic needs. Both IDEA and state statues set standards for transition services, which can help students obtain community experiences, employment training, and daily living skills. Our state, for example, requires that school districts help older students with "continuing education, developing skills for self-management of medical needs, and developing skills necessary for seeking, obtaining, and maintaining jobs."[76]

When to start transition planning

IDEA-97 required that transition planning begin with the IEP in effect on a student's 14th birthday. IDEA-04 changed this requirement to age 16. We believe, and the GAO agrees,[77] that waiting until age 16 to start transition planning is too late. Most students start high school at age 14, and that is the time to start thinking about what courses the student should take and what services the student will need to prepare for life after high school, whether it is college admission, vocational training, or independent living. By age 16, a student is usually halfway through high school and by then it might be difficult to adjust the course of study that will lead the student in the direction of his or her vision for the future.

Fortunately, IDEA-04 does not specify a minimum age for starting transition planning. Some states, such as Georgia, require that a transition plan be in place before a student enters ninth grade or reaches the age of 16, whichever comes first. Even if your state does not require it, by the ninth grade your child's IEP should include at least a brief discussion of transition and identify possible transition services.

Transition planning meeting

State laws vary in their particulars, but parents, the student, or the school district can request a transition planning meeting separate from an IEP meeting. Although most students on IEPs don't need a formal transition planning meeting, if a student's disability is significant or needs are complex, having a separate meeting allows more time to focus on the details of a transition plan than when it is combined with an IEP meeting. Usually, a formal transition planning meeting is composed of the student's IEP Team plus any specialists from outside agencies who might be knowledgeable about the available resources that can assist with the student's transition. Ideally, there should be at least two planning meetings: an initial one to create a list of assessments to determine transition needs and, once the assessments are completed, a second meeting to go over the findings and formulate the transition plan. If appropriate, the student should be involved throughout the planning discussions and meetings.

The courses and activities needed to prepare for a successful transition should be based on the student's interests, preferences, and goals for life after high school. To that end, one of the best aids for transition planning is a well-thought-out vision statement, such as described in Chapter 6, "The IEP."

Transition assessments

Assessments are an important part of transition planning for some students. The assessments can help a student's Team determine the courses, vocational training, life skills instruction, or related services that the student will need during the remainder of his or her publicly funded education. In addition to identifying abilities, strengths, and weaknesses, transition assessments should identify interests, determine appropriate levels of instruction, and recommend appropriate accommodations and services that will help with the transition process.

To decide what assessments are needed, the Team should begin with a review of existing information about the student. Most of this information should already be part of the student's IEP, such as testing data and present levels of educational performance (PLEP), supplemented by the student's vision statement or an interview. Based on that review, the Team then draws up a list of assessments appropriate for the student. These assessments can be in a variety of areas, such as educational, psychological, or medical, as well as vocational, independent living, or social and pragmatic language skills.

VOCATIONAL ASSESSMENT

If a student's current interests and vision for the future indicate that work experience rather than post-secondary education is the goal, then a vocational assessment will determine what type of work and possible training are appropriate. Most school districts provide access to a vocational assessment specialist to test a student and consult with the Team. If you believe that a vocational assessment is necessary and your district refuses to perform one, you should seek the assistance of an independent evaluator.

A complete vocational assessment covers a variety of areas such as manual dexterity, coordination, and fine motor skills. This will determine vocational strengths and limitations. An assessment should also include an interest inventory, observations by parents and teachers, and evaluations of the student in unpaid internships or paid work experience. Any data that can help form a picture of what the student might want to do or be successful doing will better inform the Team.

INDEPENDENT LIVING SKILLS ASSESSMENT

Some students, due to issues with intellectual impairments, physical impairments, or significant executive functioning deficits, will need to have an assessment of their independent living skills. Schools often contract for this evaluation as they seldom have staff trained in this area. Most valid assessments include observations at a weekend site so that a true picture emerges of a student's real-life skills in a residential setting. Areas usually addressed in these evaluations are activities of daily living (ADLs), money management, and social skills, especially with peers.

SOCIAL SKILLS AND PRAGMATIC LANGUAGE ASSESSMENT

A social skills and pragmatic language assessment may be appropriate for students on the autism spectrum. Even people with higher functioning autism often have difficulty understanding other people's perspectives and knowing how to start and maintain social interactions appropriately. These are problems that can significantly impact everyday life activities and relationships in the workplace. This assessment is generally performed by special education professionals, speech and language pathologists, or school psychologists.

A social skills and pragmatic language assessment covers three areas: the ability to understand other people's perspectives, the ability to initiate and maintain interactions and respond appropriately to other people, and the ability to understand basic and complex emotions. This information is gathered through a combination of parent and teacher questionnaires, observation, and clinical interaction. Knowing the level at which a student understands social interaction and uses pragmatic language is important to helping that student develop stronger interpersonal and job skills. This assessment can also help with placement in the most appropriate living and working environment.

The transition plan

Once the relevant assessments are complete, it is time to prepare a written transition plan. In many states the transition plan is created by the student's Team. Other states place the responsibility for developing the transition plan on representatives from agencies assisting with the transition, sometimes with assistance from the student's Team. The plan must contain specific objectives, start and end dates for services, and name the people or organizations responsible for insuring that the objectives are met. Once created, a transition plan should be revised at least once yearly as long as the student is receiving special education services.

In creating a transition plan, the Team needs to consider many facets of a young person's life beyond academics. Does the student want to attend college, a vocational school, work at a job, live independently, or live in a supported situation? The goals and services in a transition plan should be based on a student's transition assessments and reflect the student's post-secondary goals as expressed in the student's vision statement.

In addition, the Team needs to consider health care, transportation, and community experiences. For example, can a student administer his or her own medication, take public transportation, get a driver's license and drive a car, fill out a job application, do volunteer or paid work, or participate in community activities? Many students with special needs will require help in these areas in order to become independent adults, so it is critical to consider a variety of possible services such as occupational and physical therapy, speech and language therapy, remediation in reading, writing, and math skills, counseling, and travel training. The services should be meaningful to the student's goals and ideally provide motivation for the student to complete his or her education. In addition, the Team needs to consider how the entire family will participate in implementing these goals.

THE GRADUATION GAME

Graduation means an exit from high school and, for a student on an IEP, the acceptance of a diploma means an end to special education services. If a student hasn't received appropriate transition planning and services or hasn't made sufficient progress in meeting his or her transition goals, however, parents may want to consider refusing the diploma. Hearing decisions in many states have determined that a school district cannot end its special education obligations in these circumstances even though a student has completed the credits required for graduation and passed state mandated examinations.

These decisions have required school districts to either extend special education eligibility or pay for compensatory education even after awarding a diploma.[78]

Regardless of how hearing decisions interpret the law, there is a significant financial benefit for schools to end their obligation to provide special education services. This presents an incentive for schools to devise different and creative ways to move a struggling student along the path to graduation. We personally experienced inflated grades and overly optimistic progress reports that said our son was meeting his IEP goals when he wasn't. Our director of special education even offered to give our son credit for the time he would have spent in the resource room, a common practice, but one that is often suggested in place of academic courses.

We have observed that some school districts play this graduation game by adopting low graduation standards to move students out of the system. Since most states allow school districts to set their own graduation requirements, the districts can legally reduce the number of required credits, lower performance criteria, or substitute a different course for a student who might have difficulty passing a required one. This can create widely varying graduation standards among schools. In Massachusetts, a survey conducted by the state's department of education found that the number of credits required for graduation across 226 school districts varied from 60 credits to 150 credits.[79] Many of these standards do not include enough credits or the right kind of core classes to enable a student to apply to a four-year college. If a student is not on a college path then this may not be an issue, and of course, a student can always elect to take additional courses if he or she wishes. But a low graduation standard can also be used as a tool to remove a student from a district's special education obligations by forcing that student to graduate before he or she is ready.

Forced graduation

We discovered first hand the problem that low graduation standards can present for a student who has aspirations to attend college. Although our town is one of the five most affluent towns in Massachusetts in per capita income, the department of education survey revealed that our school district was among those with the very lowest standards for graduation. According to the data, at the time of the survey only five school districts in the state required fewer credits to graduate.

By contrast, the ten towns in the state with the lowest per capita income all had higher graduation standards. Compared to the state's recommended curriculum,* our district's standard only requires two years of math instead of four, two years of science instead of three, and no foreign language at all. Even though the survey was conducted more than ten years ago, as of this writing our district maintains this exceptionally low standard.

This became an issue when our district attempted to use its low standard to force our son to graduate before he had earned enough credits to apply to college. The situation developed because after eight years in the public schools, he was behind academically. Upon transferring to a private special education high school, he spent most of the first year making up for his previous lack of academic progress. It was only during his second year that he was able to fully concentrate on courses required for college admission, meaning that it was going to take a total of five years to complete his high school education. We had made the possibility of an additional year clear to the school district in the settlement agreement that we had reached with them two years earlier. It was also written into his yearly IEPs that his most important transition goal was to earn enough credits to attend a four-year college.

In spite of this, the school sent our son a letter in the fall of his fourth year in high school "congratulating" him on his hard work and his expected graduation the following June. The graduation and diploma, of course, would be from the town's high school, an institution he had never set foot in. The letter neglected to mention that his right to special education services would end with the acceptance of their diploma. Soon, the school staff started calling, asking how our son wanted his name spelled on his diploma and to have him fitted for a graduation gown.

At that spring's annual Team meeting, the district's director of special education attended and informed us that an additional year of high school "was not an option." Shortly after that we received a letter stating that our son would have to graduate. This was despite his lack of credits for college admission and despite the fact that his

---

*   The Massachusetts Department of Education promotes what it calls "MassCore," a recommended program of studies for high school students designed to prepare them for college or the workplace. MassCore includes four years of English, four years of math, three years of a lab-based science, three years of history, and two years of the same foreign language.[80]

IEP included the transition goal of getting an education adequate to prepare him for admission to a four-year college.

In order to prevent a diploma from being issued by the school district that year, we had to file another hearing request. At issue was forcing our son to graduate before he had fulfilled his transition goals. Our position was that adequate transition services included the opportunity to prepare for college. Ultimately, we reached a settlement with our district in which it agreed to pay for a portion of the extra year required to complete our son's education. Our case was strong because our son's transition goals were clear in his IEP. There have been similar cases in Massachusetts in which hearing officers ruled that accumulating required credits and passing state exams is not enough if a school does not provide adequate transition planning and services as required by IDEA.[81]

ALTERNATIVE DIPLOMAS AND GRADUATION CERTIFICATES

Schools can offer students on IEPs different kinds of exit documents that require a less rigorous curriculum than that required for a regular high school diploma. These include alternative diplomas, which go by names such as an IEP diploma or vocational diploma. Some schools offer certificates of completion or certificates of attendance. None of these documents end special education or transition services; only earning a regular high school diploma or "exceeding the age of eligibility for a free appropriate public education under state law,"[82] will do that. These alternative exit documents can be an appropriate solution for some students, but you should be aware that they can flag the graduate as a special education student and may limit that student's options for the future.

While alternative diplomas and certificates recognize that a student with a disability may be working to different standards than other students, they also indicate that the recipient may not have had full access to the general education curriculum. An alternative diploma or certificate may not be recognized as qualifying for attendance at a community college, vocational school, or enlistment in the armed forces without additional testing or certification. They can also indicate to potential employers that a job applicant has special needs or learning disabilities. Each state has different standards for diplomas and certificates, so check with your department of education to see what your state permits schools to offer.

WHAT PARENTS CAN DO

Here is a list of suggestions on how you can use the information in this chapter:

- Begin transition discussions with your Team by the time your child enters his or her freshman year in high school, usually by age 14. Start looking at post high school options, such as vocational training, internships, or further education, and have the Team write a transition plan into your child's IEP. Although the current IDEA standard requires these discussions to begin no later than age 16, this may be too late. Be sure to update the plan yearly until either graduation or your child exceeds the age of eligibility for special education in your state.

- Once your child begins high school, research your school's graduation requirements. We found our school's requirements in the high school handbook. Study the requirements carefully and plan which courses your child will need for a successful transition from high school to adult life. If further education is a goal, make sure he or she earns enough credits to apply to an appropriate college. Once your child accepts a regular high school diploma, your child's right to special education or transition services ends.

- Request separate transition planning meetings if your child's situation is complex. This allows for a more in-depth discussion, a more detailed plan, and a better chance for success.

- If academic credit is offered for resource room time, be sure to ask about the details. Will specialized instruction or counseling be offered, or will this period be unstructured free time? Consider how this option will advance your child's goals for the future. Keep in mind that the time spent in school learning is fleeting and precious.

- If your Team doesn't feel that your child can meet the course standards for a regular high school diploma, ask the following:

- ○ What accommodations and services are in the IEP that would help your child meet the same requirements as other students receiving a standard diploma?

- ○ Would staying in school until he or she reaches the maximum age of eligibility in your state allow your child to earn a standard diploma?

- ○ Would any form of alternative diploma or certificate be appropriate for your child's level of performance and would earning it give your child the skills to lead an independent life?

Be aware that an exit document other than a standard diploma does not end special education services, and that they can continue until your child reaches the maximum age of eligibility.

- Explore all transition options for your child, because not everyone goes to a four-year college. There are many post high school experiences that a student can have, such as a community college, volunteer work, vocational training, or adult education. When a student with disabilities has proper transition planning and services, the opportunities for additional education and work are greatly enhanced.

- Request a vocational assessment if your child would prefer employment rather than further education after high school. The assessment should be performed by a vocational assessment specialist and should provide direction about possible career paths and employment opportunities, as well as provide information about performance in skill areas.

- Likewise, request an independent living skills assessment, if appropriate, to determine what supports are needed for the student to live on his or her own after high school.

AFTERWORD

As we complete our manuscript, we have the pleasure of knowing that our son is just weeks away from graduating from a selective four-year college where he created a major in which he studied English literature and read ancient Greek and Latin, all disciplines that require a great deal of writing as well as critical thinking. This achievement would not have been possible if we hadn't persevered in our efforts to obtain an appropriate education for him. It was the hardest task we have ever undertaken, but it has been the most rewarding one. We hope that the information we have presented in this book, as well as the story of our own successes and failures and what we learned from them, will prove similarly rewarding for you.

TEST SCORE CONVERSIONS

The following table compares standard scores, scaled scores, percentile rank, and their relative grade level equivalents* with their accepted psychometric descriptions.

Standard Score	Scaled Score	Percentile Rank	Grade Level Equivalent	Description
130–150	16–19	98–99.9	+ 6 or higher	Very Superior
121–129	14–15	92–97	+4	Superior
111–120	12–13	76–91	+2	High Average
90–110	8–11	25–75	Grade Level	Average
80–89	6–7	9–23	–2	Low Average
70–79	4–5	2–7	–4	Borderline
55–69	1–3	1–2	–6 or lower	Mildly Impaired
40–54	n/a	Less than 1	n/a	Moderately Impaired
25–39	n/a	n/a	n/a	Severely Impaired
Less than 25	n/a	n/a	n/a	Profoundly Impaired

*While grade equivalent scores are generally not as accurate in measuring performance as standard scores or percentile rank, they are more easily understood. If a student is performing one or more years below his or her grade level in an academic or skill area, it is a reason for parents to ask questions and possibly arrange for more testing to find out why.

SPECIAL EDUCATION GLOSSARY

Special education is full of confusing acronyms and references to obscure laws and court cases. We try to use acronyms in the text as little as possible, but certain uses are unavoidable. Since you will encounter many acronyms and specialized terms in your child's journey through special education, we have compiled the following list of the most common terms and acronyms.

504 PLAN

An alternative to an IEP sometimes offered by schools to students with disabilities who do not meet special education eligibility standards. The 504 Plan is named after Section 504 of the Rehabilitation Act of 1973, a law preventing discrimination against people with disabilities. It guarantees that students with disabilities have access to the school building and school activities. Under Section 504, the definition of disability is broader than under IDEA. Unlike IDEA, Section 504 does not require a written plan similar to an IEP, and it guarantees a student only an education comparable to the education that students without disabilities receive. This means that a student may have fewer rights and protections under Section 504 than under IDEA. A 504 Plan is sometimes called an "Individualized Accommodations Plan," or IAP.

ADA (AMERICANS WITH DISABILITIES ACT)

The ADA is a law passed by Congress in 1990 that provides individuals with disabilities protection from discrimination in employment, public services and transportation, public accommodations, and telecommunications. This law was strengthened in 2008 by the passage of the Americans With Disabilities Act Amendments Act (ADAAA). The ADAAA also served to expand and clarify the definition of disabilities under Section 504 of The Rehabilitation Act of 1973.

ADL (ACTIVITIES OF DAILY LIVING)

ADLs are the things people do in daily life. These are usually self-care activities, such as feeding oneself, bathing, dressing, grooming, or working. The ability or inability to perform ADLs is often used as a measurement of the functional status of a person with disabilities.

APE (ADAPTED PHYSICAL EDUCATION)

APE is physical education modified to meet the needs of a student who has a physical impairment or delays in motor development.

ASSESSMENT

In special education, an assessment is an evaluation to determine the existence or extent of a disability. An assessment can be in academic areas, social/emotional behaviors, or physical ability. The methodology of an assessment can include standardized tests, observations, and/or interviews.

AT (ASSISTIVE TECHNOLOGY)

AT is any piece of equipment, off the shelf or customized, used to maintain or improve the capabilities of a student with disabilities. Assistive technology can be as simple as a special pencil grip or as sophisticated as speech recognition software.

ATA (ASSISTIVE TECHNOLOGY ACT)

The ATA is a law passed in 2004 that established programs to help with the purchase of assistive technology and to support the transition from school to the workforce for students with disabilities.

CONTINUUM OF ALTERNATIVE PLACEMENTS

The range of placements where a student on an IEP can receive special education services, from the least to the most restrictive environments. See also LRE.

DIRECT SERVICES

Special education services that consist of instruction provided directly to the student. These may be provided in a regular education classroom or a separate special education classroom, in a group setting or individually. See also Indirect services and Related services.

DISABILITY

Generally defined under Section 504 and the Americans with Disabilities Act as an impairment that substantially affects one or more major life activities. IDEA defines multiple categories of disability that qualify under its provisions, such as autism, developmental delay, hearing impairment, and specific learning disabilities in reading, writing, and math calculation.

DISCOVERY

A process for parties in a dispute to request and share information before a due process hearing. State special education laws vary, but IDEA requires that the parties disclose all evaluations and resulting recommendations no less than five business days prior to the hearing in which these evaluations and recommendations will be used as evidence. A hearing officer has the option of changing the deadline, however. The sooner discovery is completed, the sooner a hearing can take place.

DOE (DEPARTMENT OF EDUCATION)

The DOE is what most states call the agency that supervises the public schools in that state. The federal department of education is referred to as the USDOE.

DUE PROCESS HEARING

A legal process used by parents and school districts to resolve disputes. It is an administrative proceeding similar to a civil trial and is generally a last resort when all other attempts to solve a problem have failed. IDEA requires all states that accept federal funding for special education to make a due process hearing available.

EAHCA OR EHA (EDUCATION FOR ALL HANDICAPPED CHILDREN ACT)

A law passed by Congress in 1975 to prevent discrimination against students with disabilities and to guarantee them the right to a free appropriate public education (FAPE). In 1990 the law was reauthorized and renamed the Individuals With Disabilities Education Act (IDEA).

ESEA (ELEMENTARY AND SECONDARY EDUCATION ACT)
ESEA, a law passed in 2001, is better known as No Child Left Behind (NCLB). It requires that all schools accepting Title I funding from the federal government be accountable for the academic performance of all students. Title I is the section of ESEA that provides funding for schools with a significant population of students from low-income families to help the students meet state academic standards.

ESY (EXTENDED SCHOOL YEAR)
ESY refers to special education services that are provided during school holidays and summer vacations to prevent academic, social, or behavioral regression.

FAPE (FREE APPROPRIATE PUBLIC EDUCATION)
FAPE means that special education services are provided at public expense and under public supervision and direction, that the services meet all state and federal requirements, and comply with a student's IEP. All students on IEPs are guaranteed FAPE by law.

FBA (FUNCTIONAL BEHAVIORAL ASSESSMENT)
An FBA determines how certain situations affect a student with a suspected behavior problem. The purpose of this assessment is to identify particular events or an environment that initiates a problem behavior with the goal of eliminating or modifying the "trigger" event. An FBA will often lead to the development of a behavior intervention plan (BIP).

FERPA (FAMILY EDUCATIONAL RIGHTS AND PRIVACY ACT)
FERPA is a federal law that protects the privacy of student records and assures parents of the right to inspect their child's school records.

GL (GRADE LEVEL) OR GE (GRADE EQUIVALENT)
A term appearing in many evaluations and IEPs to designate the level at which a student is performing. For example, a tenth grade student who is performing in a subject area at a sixth grade level (or equivalent) is behind his or her peers, while a third grade student performing at a sixth grade level is considered advanced. Ideally, a student's tested grade level should consistently match or exceed the student's actual grade level.

HEARING
See due process hearing.

IAP (INDIVIDUALIZED ACCOMMODATION PLAN)
A document that details specific strategies and practices used to help parents and teachers meet a child's learning needs under the terms of Section 504 of the Rehabilitation Act of 1973 and the Americans with Disabilities Act. Often used as an alternative label for a 504 Plan.

IDEA (INDIVIDUALS WITH DISABILITIES EDUCATION ACT)
IDEA is the federal law that prohibits discrimination against students with disabilities and guarantees them the right to a free appropriate public education (FAPE). Sometimes this acronym is followed by a number, such as IDEA-97, which refers to a specific revision of the law according to the revision date, i.e., 1997.

IEE (INDEPENDENT EDUCATIONAL EVALUATION)
An evaluation conducted by a qualified professional not employed by your child's school district. If you disagree with a school's evaluation, you have the right to request an independent evaluation at public expense.

IEP (INDIVIDUALIZED EDUCATION PROGRAM)
Sometimes called an "Individualized Education Plan," the IEP is a document that specifies what services and placement a student in special education will receive each year.

IEP TEAM

The group of education professionals and parents charged by IDEA to make special education decisions about a student. This includes eligibility, testing, development of the IEP, and services.

INCLUSION

Providing services to a student on an IEP in the general education classroom. Sometimes called "mainstreaming."

INDIRECT SERVICES

Special education services not provided directly to a student on an IEP. These might include consultation provided by specialists to parents or teachers. See also Direct services and Related services.

INTERVENTION SPECIALIST OR INCLUSION SPECIALIST

A teacher with specialized knowledge about educating students with disabilities in the mainstream classroom. See also special education liaison.

LD (LEARNING DISABILITY)

IDEA defines specific learning disabilities that may qualify a student for special education services.

LEA (LOCAL EDUCATIONAL AGENCY)

IDEA requires that a member of the local educational agency be part of a student's IEP Team. In most cases, the LEA is the school district.

LIAISON

See special education liaison.

LRE (LEAST RESTRICTIVE ENVIRONMENT)

The IDEA mandate that all children with disabilities be educated with nondisabled peers to the "maximum extent possible." Also see LRE continuum and mainstream.

LRE CONTINUUM

The range of placement options for a student in special education. Schools must consider a continuum of alternative placement options to meet the unique needs of a student with disabilities and not just assume that a mainstream classroom, even with aids and accommodations, is always an appropriate environment.

MAINSTREAM

The general education classroom setting.

MEDIATION

A facilitated negotiation to resolve a dispute between parents and a school district. Mediation is usually seen as a more timely and cost-effective way to settle problems than a due process hearing. IDEA requires that mediation be provided at no cost to the parties involved. Participation in a mediation is voluntary.

NCLB (NO CHILD LEFT BEHIND)

While not specifically a special education law, NCLB does mandate that students with disabilities be held to the same high academic standards as their non-disabled peers. This means that most students with disabilities take the same tests (although with accommodations, if appropriate) and meet the same annual yearly progress goals as all other students. If a student is unable to take a standardized test due to the nature of his or her disability, then the student can participate in an alternative assessment specified by that student's IEP Team. See also ESEA.

OT (OCCUPATIONAL THERAPY)

OT is a related service in which the therapist works with a student to enhance that student's fine and/or gross motor skills and ability to perform the activities of daily life. While the therapies are mostly physical, they often address various cognitive and sensory integration issues.

PAC (PARENT ADVISORY COUNCIL)

See SEPAC.

PLAAFP

See PLEP.

PLACEMENT

The school environment or program is referred to as a "placement," that is, where your child is educated. Placement is an important part of the IEP.

PLACEMENT PENDING APPEAL

See stay put.

PLEP, PLOP, OR PLAAFP

The acronyms refer respectively to present levels of educational performance, present levels of performance, and present levels of academic achievement and functional performance. PLEP is used to describe the current, relevant information about a student. This assessment, obtained from teachers, evaluations, and parents, among other sources, is used to determine an IEP's goals and services for the student. This term is also sometimes referred to as PLOP, or PLAAFP.

PLOP

See PLEP.

POST-SECONDARY EDUCATION

Formal education or training beyond high school.

PRO SE

Latin term meaning "for oneself." A parent who represents him or herself in a due process hearing instead of using an attorney is a *pro se* party.

PT (PHYSICAL THERAPY)

PT is therapy that specializes in correcting physical impairments and promoting mobility. A physical therapist can help a student with walking, running, jumping, and similar activities.

PWN (PRIOR WRITTEN NOTICE)

Schools are required to give prior written notice to parents of an impending action the school is proposing to take or not take, such as placement in a particular educational setting, or refusing a parent's request to evaluate a child for learning disabilities. The PWN must describe the action the school is taking (or refusing to take) and explain the reasons for the decision.

RELATED SERVICES

Services that enable a student with disabilities to benefit from special education. These are defined by IDEA to include transportation; occupational, speech and language, and physical therapies; counseling; and medical services, among others, to support the student's education. See also direct services and indirect services.

RESOURCE ROOM

A room separate from the regular education classroom where students in special education can go to receive individualized instruction and other assistance.

SECTION 504

See 504 Plan.

SEPAC (SPECIAL EDUCATION PARENT ADVISORY COUNCIL)

SEPAC is a group of parents of students in special education who meet, usually monthly, to hear lectures by professionals involved in special education and discuss issues that the parents face. SEPACs are mandated in many states for every school district. Also sometimes shortened to "Parent Advisory Council," or PAC.

SPECIAL EDUCATION LIAISON

The title given the person who supervises the services provided a student on an IEP. This person typically runs Team meetings and writes drafts of the IEP. In some school districts the liaison is called an "intervention specialist" or "inclusion specialist."

SPECIFIC LEARNING DISABILITY

Defined by IDEA as a particular disorder that may qualify a student for special education. This includes an impaired ability to "listen, think, speak, read, write, spell, or perform mathematical calculations."

STAY PUT

A safeguard written into IDEA that requires the school to maintain (or "stay put") a student's current services or placement while a dispute with parents is being resolved. This means that if a school wants to reduce a student's services or remove a student from a special education placement and the parents disagree with this change, the school cannot make the change until the disagreement is resolved. The formal legal term for stay put is "placement pending appeal."

TRANSITION AND TRANSITION SERVICES

A coordinated set of activities for a student in special education designed to help that student move from high school to post-secondary activities, such as college, vocational education, employment, independent living, or community participation. Starting no later than the IEP in effect on the student's 16th birthday (earlier in some states), the IEP must include a transition plan to identify and develop goals needed to accomplish a successful transition based on the individual's needs. Transition services coordinate the student's transition and continue until high school graduation or the student exceeds the age of eligibility for special education (between 18 and 21 depending on the state), whichever comes first.

TRANSITION PLAN

The transition plan is a document that lays out the goals and services needed to help a student make the transition from school to post-secondary life—whether a job, vocational training, college, independent living, or supported living environment—when that student has complex special needs.

State laws vary about how a transition plan is developed and its relationship to the special education process, but in general the plan should be based on the student's needs and preferences, and should reflect the student's goals as expressed in the student's IEP vision statement. A transition plan, like the IEP, must include specific objectives, start and end dates for recommended services, and the people or organizations responsible for insuring that the objectives are met.

VISION STATEMENT

A section of the IEP in most states (but not required by IDEA) expressing the concerns, hopes, and future goals of the student for the next one to five years. Parents will have to write this for a young student, while older students can write about their hopes and dreams for the future beyond high school based on their preferences and interests. A well-articulated vision statement can assist the IEP Team in writing appropriate goals to help the student attain his or her desired outcomes for future education, employment, and independent living.

SPECIAL EDUCATION RESOURCES

During our years in special education we searched for resources that could help us with parenting, school, and a greater understanding of disabilities and special education law. The following is our list of worthwhile books and online resources that cover the subjects discussed in this book and why we think they may be helpful to you.

GENERAL

From Emotions to Advocacy, 2nd edition
Pam Wright and Pete Wright (2006) Hartfield, VA: Harbor House Law Press

> If you purchase only one other book on special education, this should be the one. Pam and Pete Wright are in the forefront of helping parents understand and deal effectively with special education. The WrightsLaw website (see the section General Special Education Websites) is likewise one of the best Internet resources for parents.

Negotiating the Special Education Maze: A Guide for Parents and Teachers, 2nd edition
Winifred Anderson, Stephen Chitwood and Deidre Hayden (1990) Rockville, MD: Woodbine House

> While dated, this book contains a lot of useful information about the special education process. The biggest flaw is the authors' assumption that the school will always have the best interests of the child in mind and will always try to have a productive partnership with parents. Therefore, while the book accurately describes mediation and due process hearings, it doesn't really prepare readers for why they may need them.

Learning Disabilities From a Parent's Perspective
Kim Glenchur (2003) San Francisco: Pince-Nez Press

> Researched like a graduate thesis with exhaustive quotes and footnotes, this book covers a lot of ground and does it accurately. Long quotations from primary sources make this a difficult read in places.

Special Needs Advocacy Resource Book
Weinfeld, Rich and Michelle Davis, Waco, TX, Prufrock Press, Inc. 2008

> Covers special education from the viewpoint of an advocate. If you study this book carefully, you may develop some of the advocacy skills.

The IEP

Writing Measurable IEP Goals and Objectives
Barbara D. Bateman and Cynthia M. Herr (2006) Verona, WI: Attainment Company
> This is a clear and concise guide to one of the most important parts of the IEP. It contains useful examples that you can follow.

How Well Does Your IEP Measure Up?
Diane Twachtman-Cullen and Jennifer Twachtman-Reilly (2011) San Francisco: Jossey-Bass
> A step-by-step guide to writing IEPs by two speech and language pathologists. It contains sample goals, objectives and recommended teaching strategies.

All About IEPs
Peter W. D. Wright, Pamela Darr Wright and Sandra Webb O'Connor (2010) Hartfield, VA: Harbor House Law Press
> Providing answers to more than 200 frequently asked questions about the IEP process with emphasis on how special education laws affect the development and implementation of an IEP, this is best as a supplementary text rather than a main resource.

Quick Reference Guide to the Diagnostic Criteria from DSM-IV-TR
American Psychiatric Association (2000) Arlington, VA: American Psychiatric Association
> The DSM contains the standards for classifying mental disorders accepted by the American Psychiatric Association. The quick reference contains most of the accepted descriptions of the disabilities defined by IDEA. If your child's IEP contains a diagnosis described in this book, this is a way to check its accuracy. While expensive relative to how much you may need to use it, most public libraries will have a copy that you can refer to as needed.

Legal

The Complete IEP Guide: How to Advocate for Your Special Ed Child, 7th edition
Lawrence M. Siegel (2011) Berkeley, CA: Nolo
> This is a comprehensive guide to special education and IEPs from a legal point of view. The completeness is both a strength and a weakness, as there is so much information it can be hard to find exactly what you are looking for so it is best used as a reference. There are few books that cover the whole area of special education better. Note that Nolo publishes multiple versions of this book with slightly different titles and slightly altered text. One version appears to be as good as another.

Wrightslaw: Special Education Law, 2nd edition
Peter W. D. Wright and Pamela Darr Wright (2007) Hartfield, VA: Harbor House Law Press
> A complete, annotated text of IDEA and supporting special education laws and regulations, including descriptions of and commentaries on important cases pertaining to special education. You may not initially think you need a book with this amount of detail, but you'll be amazed at how often you start to refer to it.

Testing

Straight Talk about Psychological Testing for Kids
Ellen Braaten and Gretchen Felopulos (2004) New York: Guilford Press
> The authors provide very clear explanations of how psychological testing works and how testing can identify specific learning disabilities. They discuss the issues of interpreted scores, deciphering jargon-filled reports, and making sure that a report contains useful recommendations, as well as how to choose the right professional to conduct tests.

Measuring Instructional Results, 3rd edition
Robert F. Mager (1997) Atlanta, GA: CEP
> Written for teachers, this book describes how to measure whether or not a student is meeting his or her instructional goals. This book's value for parents is in explaining how Teams can create standards by which a student's academic IEP goals will be measured.

TACTICAL ADVICE

How to Compromise With Your School District Without Compromising Your Child
Gary Mayerson (2004) New York: DRL Books
> An engaging and candid text, written by a special education lawyer who is also the parent of a child with special needs. Full of first-hand accounts of dealing with school districts. Many of these accounts read like verbatim descriptions of interactions we have had with our school district, illustrating how problems in special education are widespread.

Disability Deception: Lies Disability Educators Tell and How Parents Can Beat Them at Their Own Game!
JoAnn Collins (2007) Bradley, Il: JoAnn Collins Publishing
> If you can look beyond the multitude of typographical and proofreading errors in this self-published book, you will get a real education in the ways that the special education system prevents students from getting FAPE. While we don't agree with all the tactics the author advocates, she is clearly someone who has been through the process and has genuine insights to share.

The Art of War
Sun Tzu (2003) New York: Barnes and Noble Classics
> An unfortunate truth is that obtaining FAPE for your child often requires many of the same skills and mindset that a general uses on the battlefield.

GENERAL SPECIAL EDUCATION WEBSITES

WrightsLaw
www.wrightslaw.com
> Home page of the "go to" website for parents in special education. Many of the articles that appear on this site are excerpts from Pete and Pamela Wright's books. In addition, there are articles by guest columnists, links to resources, directories of information, and updates as the laws change. You can also sign up for an informative email newsletter.

LD OnLine
www.ldonline.org/parents
> Describing itself as "The world's leading website on learning disabilities and ADHD," LD OnLine contains many links to articles and resources covering a wide variety of learning disabilities and special education issues.

National Center for Learning Disabilities (NCLD)
www.ncld.org
> NCLD is "committed to ensuring that all students with learning disabilities graduate from high school with a standard diploma, prepared for college and the workplace." The website is well organized with sections that include descriptions of different types of learning disabilities, information for parents, and a resource locator for various types of resources pertaining to learning disabilities.

Great schools
www.greatschools.org/special-education.topic?content=1541
> This is the special education topic page for learning disabilities for Great Schools, a non-profit organization set up to help parents advocate for their child's education. It links to many informative articles and is frequently updated.

Online Degrees.Org
www.onlinedegrees.org/top-40-special-education-blogs
> With links to the "top 40" special education blogs as compiled by OnlineDegrees.org, this website is intended as a resource for teachers. Many of the blogs contain worthwhile information for parents too.

Learning Disabilities Association of America
www.ldanatl.org
> With links for parents, teachers, and adults with learning disabilities, this is a good place to start research of almost any kind.

US Department of Education Office of Special Education Programs (OSEP)
www.ed.gov/about/offices/list/osers/osep/index.html?src=mr
> The OSEP website contains links to many government sites supporting special education and students with disabilities.

Parent-Focused Websites
Concord SEPAC
http://concordspedpac.org
> This website is worth browsing for its general information on special education, list of resources, and description of state and federal disability laws. Concord SEPAC is an excellent example of what a parent's advocacy organization should be and how it can serve the special education community.

Parent Technical Assistance Center Network
www.parentcenternetwork.org
> This is the home page of the Parent Technical Assistance Center Network website. The Parent Centers, located in all parts of the country, provide training, information, and free advocacy help. The website contains links that will help you locate a group in your area.

Resource Locator Websites
Yellow Pages for Kids with Disabilities
www.yellowpagesforkids.com
> Yellow Pages for Kids with Disabilities, sponsored by Wrightslaw, is a locator for special education resources in all areas of the country. Just click on your state on the map and you get an A to Z listing of advocates, therapists, tutoring services, and just about any other resource you might need.

US Department of Education: Education Resource Organizations Directory
http://wdcrobcolp01.ed.gov/Programs/EROD/org_list.cfm?category_ID=SPT
> This is a government-maintained directory of disability resources organized by state.

National Disability Rights Network (NDRN)
www.ndrn.org
> NDRN is the non-profit membership organization for the federally mandated Protection and Advocacy Systems and Client Assistance Programs. Together, these are the largest group of providers of legally based advocacy services to people with disabilities in the United States. The home page contains links to locate services in your area.

Council of Parent Attorneys and Advocates (COPAA)
www.copaa.org
> The COPAA website enables you to locate attorneys, advocates, and other professionals who belong to the organization and advocate on behalf of children with disabilities. It contains guides on how to select an appropriate professional for your needs.

National Comprehensive Center for Teaching Quality
http://mb2.ecs.org/reports/reporttq.aspx?id=1542&map=0
> This is a website sponsored by the Education Commission of the States, where you can research the certification requirements for teachers and school specialists in your state.

IDEA AND FEDERAL SPECIAL EDUCATION LAW WEBSITES
Federal Register
www.federalregister.gov/articles/search?conditions[term]=IDEA&commit=Go
> A website maintained by the US Department of Education that explains the federal special education laws.

IDEA
http://idea.ed.gov/explore/home
> A "one-stop shop" for resources related to IDEA and supporting regulations, the website includes the facility to search IDEA for keywords and phrases.

NOTES

The statutory provisions of IDEA are contained in 20 USC §1400 through 1482, and in many cases are explained in greater detail by the regulations in 34 CFR Part 300. In the following notes, where the regulation contains the citation referred to in the text, the authorizing statute for that regulation appears after the regulation for reference.

1. *Brown v. Bd. of Ed. Of Topeka, Shawnee Cnty., Kan.,* 347 U.S. 483, 493 (1954).

2. *Pennsylvania Ass'n for Retarded Children v. Com. Of Pa.,* 334 F. Supp. 1257, 1260 (E.D. Pa 1971).

3. Chapter 766 of the Acts and Resolves of the General Court of Massachusetts, 1972. Footnote to M.G.L c.71B.

4. *Bd. of Educ. of Hendrick Hudson Cent. Sch. Dist., Westchester Cnty. v. Rowley,* 458 U.S. 176, 195, 199 (1982).

5. "History of Special Education." Accessed on 10 November 2010 at www.answers.com/topic/history-of-special-education

6. *Anne Sullivan Macy.* Accessed on 11 October 2011 at http://en.wikipedia.org/wiki/Anne_Sullivan_Macy

7. Massachusetts law defines effective progress as "documented growth in the acquisition of knowledge and skills, including social/emotional development, within the general education program, with or without accommodations, according to chronological age and developmental expectations..." 603 C.M.R. §28.02(17). Federal regulations simply state that "Each State must ensure that FAPE is available to any individual child with a disability who needs special education and related services, even though the child has not failed or been retained in a course or grade, and is advancing from grade to grade" 34 CFR §300.101(c)(1). The authorizing statute is 20 USC §1412(a)(1)(A). The broader definition contained in the federal regulations is much more open to interpretation.

8. 20 USC §6301.

9. Parrish, T. (2006) "National and State Overview of Special Education Funding." Center for Special Education Finance. Accessed on 22 July 2011 at http://csef.air.org/presentations/KS%20SE%20presentation%203-1-06.pdf

10. Parrish, T., Harr, J., Anthony, J., Merickel, A., and Esra, P. (2003) *State Special Education Finance Systems, 1999–2000, Part 1* Palo Alto, CA: Center for Special Education Finance. Accessed on 10 September 2012 at http://csef.air.org/publications/csef/state/statpart1.pdf

11. Siegel, L. (2009) *The Complete IEP Guide,* 6th edition. Berkeley, CA: Nolo Press, p.118.

12. Reeve, C. (2002) *Nothing is Impossible: Reflections on a New Life.* New York: Random House, p.89.

13. Esack, S. (2012) "Federal Jury Awards Parent Diana Zhou $10,000 in Retaliation Claim against BASD." *The Morning Call.* Accessed on 16 August 2012 at http://articles.mcall.com/2012-08-16/news/mc-bethlehem-schools-zhou-jury-20120816_1_diana-zhou-retaliation-claim-jury-trials

14. Simon, S. (2011) "Public Schools Charge Kids for Basics, Frills." *The Wall Street Journal,* 25 May.

15. Shah, N. (2011) "Districts Hire Outsider to Trim Special Ed. Costs." *Education Week,* 25 May. Accessed on 28 March 2012 at www.edweek.org/ew/articles/2011/05/25/32futures.h30.html

16. 20 USC §1401(29).

17. 20 USC §1412(a)(1)(B)(i-ii).

18. 20 USC §1414(a)(1)(C)(i)(I). State laws may require a shorter time period.

19. 34 CFR §300.613(a). The authorizing statutes are 20 USC §1412(a)(8) and 20 USC §1417(c). This regulation is not just about evaluations; it specifies a parent's general access rights to school records, and is broadly inclusive. It gives parents the right "to inspect and review any education records relating to their children that are collected, maintained, or used by the agency."

20. The full text reads: "To the maximum extent appropriate, children with disabilities, including children in public or private institutions or other care facilities, are educated with children who are not disabled, and special classes, separate schooling, or other removal of children with disabilities from the regular educational environment occurs only when the nature or severity of the disability of a child is such that education in regular classes with the use of supplementary aids and services cannot be achieved satisfactorily" 20 USC §1412(a)(5)(A).

21. Hartmann Hartmann v. Loudoun County Board Of Education, No. 96–2809. Accessed on 23 January 2013 at http://caselaw.findlaw.com/us-4th-circuit/1089750.html

22. 34 CFR §300.115(a). The authorizing statute is 20 USC §1412(a)(5).

23. Mayerson, G. (2004) *How to Compromise With Your School District Without Compromising Your Child.* New York: DRL Press, p.103.

24. CDMAR §13A.5.05.01.06C(2).

25. Editorial (2004) "Special Needs, Common Goals." *Education Week,* 8 January, p.7.

26. US Department of Education (2004) "New No Child Left Behind Flexibility: Highly Qualified Teachers." Accessed on 5 March 2012 at www2.ed.gov/nclb/methods/teachers/hqtflexibility.html

27. Adair, J. (2007) "Special Ed Drained by Paperwork." *The Dedham Transcript,* 19 July. Accessed on 28 March 2012 at www.dailynewstranscript.com/news/x533531306

28. Wright, P. and Wright, P. (1999) *From Emotions to Advocacy,* 2nd edition. Hartfield, VA: Harbor House Press, p.41.

29. WrightsLaw (2012) "Parent/School Relationship: Marriage Without the Possibility of Divorce." Accessed on 22 July 2011 at www.wrightslaw.com/blog/?p=3647

30. Rutter, M., Bishop, D.V.M., Pine, D.S., Scott, S., *et al.* (2010) *Rutter's Child and Adolescent Psychiatry,* 5th edition. London: Wiley-Blackwell, pp.311–312.

31. WrightsLaw (2013) "Retaliation." Accessed on 21 September 2013 at www.wrightslaw.com/info/retal.index.htm

32. 34 CFR §300.305(a)(1)(i). The authorizing statute is 20 USC §1414(c)(1)(A)(i). The regulation states that "The IEP Team and other qualified professionals, as appropriate, must review existing evaluation data on the child including evaluations and information provided by the parents of the child." The term "qualified professionals" clearly includes

any school examiners and there is no reason for this information not to be part of the report.

33. Accessed on 9 December 2011 at http://myspace.aamu.edu/users/sha.li/home/StandardScores.htm

34. Bratten, E. and Felopulos, G. (2004) *Straight Talk about Psychological Testing for Kids*. New York: The Guilford Press, p.161.

35. Meyer, M. "What to Expect from an Evaluation." Accessed on 3 June 2012 at www.fetaweb.com/03/eval.expect.meyer.htm. Accessed on 10 November 2013.

36. American Psychiatric Association (2000) *Diagnostic Criteria from DSM-IV-TR*. Arlington, VA.

37. Rutter *et al. loc. cit.*

38. Alessi, G. (1998) "Diagnosis Diagnosed: A Systemic Reaction." *Professional School Psychology*, 3(2), 145–151.

39. 34 CFR §300.8(c)(12). The authorizing statutes are 20 USC §1401(3) and 20 USC §1401(30).

40. 20 USC §1414(b)(3)(C).

41. 34 CFR §300.502(a)(3)(i). The authorizing statutes are 20 USC §1415(b)(1) and 20 USC §1415(d)(2)(A).

42. 20 USC §1414(b)(3)(B).

43. 34 CFR §300.502(b)(2). The authorizing statutes are 20 USC §1415(b)(1) and 20 USC §1415(d)(2)(A).

44. Atkinson, D. (2010) "Psychologist: Newton Schools Lax on Special Education Evaluations." *The Newton Tab*, 27 January. Accessed on 27 January 2010 at www.wickedlocal.com/newton/news/x985823885/Psychologist-Newton-schools-lax-on-special-education-evaluations

45. "The assessor may recommend appropriate types of placements, but shall not recommend specific classrooms or schools" 603 CMR. §28.04(2)(c). Note that this is a state law specific to Massachusetts; IDEA does not have a similar restriction.

46. Alessi, *loc. cit.*

47. Descriptions of two landmark cases in which teachers were fired for advocating for their students can be found at: www.wrightslaw.com/info/retal.index.htm Accessed on 7 March 2012).

48. 20 USC §1414(d)(1)(A)(i)(II).

49. This behavior is described in Bateman, B.D. (1995) "Writing Individualized Education Programs (IEPs) for Success." Accessed on 20 January 2012 at www.wrightslaw.com/advoc/articles/iep.success.bateman.htm

50. 34 CFR §300.321(a). The authorizing statutes are 20 USC §1414(d)(1)(B) through (d)(1)(D).

51. 20 USC §1414(d)(2)(A).

52. 603 CMR §28.05(7). A memorandum from the State Director of Special Education dated 1 December 2006, clarifies this point further.

53. 20 USC §1414(d)(1)(A)(i)(I).

54. 20 USC §1414(d)(1)(A)(i)(IV).

55. 20 USC §1414(a)(1)(D).

56. Adapted from Batemen, B. and Herr, C. (2003) *Writing Measurable IEP Goals and Objectives*. Verona, WI: IEP Resources, pp.13–14.

57. 20 USC §1414(d)(1)(B).

58. 34 CFR §300.321(e)(1). The authorizing statute is 20 USC §1414(d)(1)(C)(iii).

59. 20 USC §1414(d)(3)(E).

60. Wright, P. (2008) "Tapes are 'Best Evidence' in Litigation." Accessed on 6 February 2012 at www.wrightslaw.com/blog/?p=63

61. 34 CFR §300.322(a). The authorizing statue is 20 USC §1415(b)(1).

62. 34 CFR §300.613. The authorizing statue is 20 USC §1415(d)(2)(D).

63. Mittnacht, M. (2011) "Memorandum on Procedures Lite." Massachusetts Department of Elementary and Secondary Education. Accessed on 29 September 2012 at www.doe.mass. edu/news/news.aspx?id=6585

64. 20 USC §1415(e)(2)(F).

65. 20 USC §1415(f)(3)(C).

66. 20 USC §1415(f)(1)(B)(i)(I).

67. 20 USC §1415(f)(2)(A).

68. 20 USC §1415(j).

69. 20 USC §1415(i)(3)(B)(i)(II). In "New School District Attorney's Fees Provision Under IDEA 2004," Jess Butler describes the court decisions. Accessed on 3 October 2012 at www.wrightslaw.com/idea/art/atty.fees.butler.htm

70. Chapter III, paragraph 2. Although the text of *The Art of War* can be translated many different ways, this particular translation captures the goal of special education litigation best.

71. 603 C.M.R. §28.05(4)(c).

72. US Department of Education, President's Commission on Excellence in Special Education (2002) *A New Era: Revitalizing Special Education for Children and Their Families*, p.12. Accessed on 22 February 2012 at http://ectacenter.org/~pdfs/calls/2010/earlypartc/revitalizing_special_education.pdf

73. United States Government Accountability Office (July 2012) *Students with Disabilities: Better Federal Coordination Could Lessen Challenges in the Transition from High School*. Report to the Ranking Member, Committee on Education and the Workforce, House of Representatives. GAO-12-594.

74. Commonwealth of Massachusetts Bureau of Special Education Appeals, BSEA # 08-5330, In Re: Dracut Public Schools, p 37. Accessed on 1 October 2012 at www.doe. mass.edu/bsea/decisions/08-5330.pdf

75. 20 USC §1414(d)(1)(A)(i)(VIII).

76. 603 CMR §28.06(4).

77. United States Government Accountability Office, *op. cit*, p.16.

78. Oberman, C. "Transition Services and The Broadening of The Special Education Mandate" cites cases from several states. Accessed on 23 February 2013 at www.caryloberman.com/articles/transition-services-and-the-broadening-of-the-special-education- mandate

79. Massachusetts Department of Education (February 2001) "Local Graduation Requirements in Massachusetts Public High Schools." Accessed on 12 March 2012 at www.doe.mass. edu/news/archive01/gradreq.pdf

80. Massachusetts Department of Elementary and Secondary Education, "What is MassCore?" Accessed on 23 February 2012 at www.doe.mass.edu/ccr/masscore

81. Hagerty, E. "Commentary on Massachusetts Special Education Decisions." Accessed on 27 February 2012 at http://cambridgepacse.org/wp-content/uploads/2011/04/Transition-Presentation-Cambridge-SEPAC-11-18-10-Handouts-p-76-to-87-2.pdf

82. 20 USC §1414(c)(5)(B)(i).

INDEX